Mt. Κοίνη

A Trail Guide

Maury Robertson/Anchorpoint Press
2443 Fillmore St. 380 2427
San Francisco, CA 94115

http://greekforeveryone.com

Mt. Koine/ Maury Robertson. —1st ed.

ISBN-10: 0-9994916-0-1
ISBN-13: 978-0-9994916-0-7

Πάτερ ἡμῶν
ὁ ἐν τοῖς οὐρανοῖς,

ἁγιασθήτω τὸ ὄνομά σου·
ἐλθέτω ἡ βασιλεία σου·
γενηθήτω τὸ θέλημά σου,

ὡς ἐν οὐρανῷ, καὶ ἐπὶ γῆς·

τὸν ἄρτον ἡμῶν τὸν ἐπιούσιον δὸς ἡμῖν σήμερον·

καὶ ἄφες ἡμῖν τὰ ὀφειλήματα ἡμῶν,
ὡς καὶ ἡμεῖς ἀφίεμεν τοῖς ὀφειλέταις ἡμῶν·

καὶ μὴ εἰσενέγκῃς ἡμᾶς εἰς πειρασμόν,
ἀλλὰ ῥῦσαι ἡμᾶς ἀπὸ τοῦ πονηροῦ.

Ὅτι σοῦ ἐστιν ἡ βασιλεία
καὶ ἡ δύναμις
καὶ ἡ δόξα
εἰς τοὺς αἰῶνας.

Ἀμήν.

Foreword

Welcome to Greek for Everyone!

Let's admit it: If learning Greek interests you, you are an odd person. You are also a brave person. Most people think of learning Greek as right up there with becoming a nuclear physicist or a rocket scientist. The average person assumes it is impossible and will never even try.

The truth is, anyone can learn Greek. This does not mean that it will be easy. Unless you are a genius, Greek will boggle your mind. There will be terrifying new terms you have never met and concepts that may take weeks to sink in. So why bother?

Because some of the best experiences of life are the the most difficult. There is a great sense of accomplishment when you do something difficult.

In 2011, my son and I climbed Half Dome in Yosemite National Park. I am not comfortable with heights, so this scared me out of my wits. It felt like I was suspended out over nothing, hanging onto those slippery cables for dear life.

Why would I put myself through that?

Because the rush I felt at the top was like nothing I have ever experienced. I faced a difficult challenge and overcame it.

In the same way, there will be times during this class when you feel like you are about to fall to your death. Hang on! Conquering Greek is worth it! Why? Because...

When You Climb Mt. Greek

You will be able to **read first century Greek documents** like the New Testament, the Septuagint, and Greek writers like Plutarch with the freshness and force of the original language.

You will have a **sophisticated understanding of grammar**. The word grammar is a dirty word in many places today. Rosetta Stone has popularized the idea of grammar-free language. This is nonsense! Grammar is our friend!

Once you master grammar, there are enormous benefits.

- You will be a **better writer and speaker**. Greek has greatly improved my writing and speaking skills, simply because I understand the rules for putting words together.

- You will have a foundation that will make **learning other languages** much easier. Once you know the rules of grammar, they apply to every language.

- If you are a student worried about **doing well on standardized tests** to get into college or grad school, Greek will help you enormously with the English section. You really cannot learn Greek well without mastering English grammar.

- This may sound strange, but Greek will even **help you think better**. Why? Because we think with language. Master grammar and your brain simply works better.

I teach the Greek that was spoken in the first century, known as *Hellenistic Greek,* or sometimes, *Koine Greek.* "Koine" (pronounced "COIN-ay") just means "common." It was the Greek spoken by the common person all over the world.

If you are interested in Modern Greek or Classical Greek, Hellenistic Greek is a good place to begin. It is not as nuanced as Classical Greek, and it is pronounced differently than Modern Greek, but it has close similarities with both so it is easy to go from one to the other.

The Challenges

Before mountain climbers begin their ascent, they study the mountain to anticipate obstacles to determine their route. As we approach Mount Κοίνη, here are some of the challenges we can anticipate.

It's a Big Mountain!

There used to be a method advertising "Greek in a Week." This is like inviting people to pack a picnic lunch to scale Everest. Mount Κοίνη is a lofty one. The top is way up in the clouds. There is no short cut, but there are ways to ascend that are less difficult than others. It can be downright fun.

In fact, the joy is in the journey. All along the way the vistas get better and better. Muscles grow stronger. Your mind is a muscle, after all, and muscles like to be exercised. The promise that Greek (or anything else) can be learned with the click of a mouse is always false. The computer may be a helpful tool, but only you can master Greek.

Strange Looking Letters

Most people look at a Greek text and are immediately intimidated by the strange looking letters. They assume this presents an insurmountable obstacle. Not so! The Greek alphabet is similar enough to the English alphabet that you will find it easy to adapt, and unlike English, Greek pronunciation is marvelously consistent. You just say what you see.

English

Believe it or not, one of the greatest obstacles to learning Greek is English. English is a strange and inconsistent language. We are so accustomed to it that we don't notice.

Greek is much more logical and consistent (and lovely) than English. Often the challenge is not that the Greek is unclear, but that discovering a way to say something in English is difficult.

Jumbled Up, Shape-Shifting Words

One thing that will strike you very quickly is that Greek word order seems all jumbled up. This is because Greek does not rely much on word order to tell us the role the words play in a sentence the way English does. Instead, Greek words change form (called "morphology") to explain how a sentence goes together to give meaning (called "syntax").

This is the greatest challenge of learning Greek.

The patterns of change are marvelously regular, even awe-inspiring once you learn to recognize them. For a while it will be overwhelming, though. Every part of speech has its own patterns of behavior that must be learned. This is why there is no way to escape grammar if you really want to learn Greek.

Terms, Terms And More Terms

As we start to describe all the changes that Greek words go through, we will need terms to describe the changes. Since there are many changes, there are many terms. I promise that you will get them mixed up, at least at first.

Nothing about Greek is difficult. It is as easy as snapping puzzle pieces together. The problem is that there are too many pieces. It is like being handed a 10,000 piece puzzle.

Along the way, you will be overwhelmed. You will feel like there are half a million pieces! This is normal. You are not stupid. You are attempting a great feat. If it were easy, everyone would do it. As someone who is getting closer to putting the puzzle together, I can assure you that it is possible. There are not as many pieces as it seems at first. When the picture starts to take shape, you will feel a rush. It is worth it!

Our Approach

Each week consists of six parts.

1. Watch a 20-30 minute video.
2. Read Mt. Κοίνη (the Greek Grammar).
3. Do some exercises in the Take a Hike! exercise book.
4. Work on vocabulary. (Learn 20 vocabulary words.)
5. Put yourself to the test. (Take the online quizzes.)
6. Stay fired up! (Meet in the live weekly session.)

Here's another.

πιστευθέντος
(being believed)

breaking it into pieces…

πιστευ θέ ντ ος

➡ θε tells me this must be an aorist passive participle.

➡ ος is the genitive singular, masculine or neuter case ending in the third declension.

So to parse πιστευθέντος we simply describe it as an aorist, passive participle, genitive, singular, masculine or neuter.

One more.

εἰπών
(saying)

Let's break it into pieces.

εἰπ ων

➡ The stem changed from λέγ to εἰπ. It is a second aorist.

➡ It uses the odd ων ending which is the active, nominative, singular, masculine form.

So to parse εἰπών we simply describe it as a second aorist, active participle, nominative, singular, masculine.

That is how you parse an aorist participle.

Now let's look at some aorist participles in sentences. Remember that the only difference in meaning will be that of aspect.

How To Use The Aorist Participle

Adjectival Participle

σὺ εἶ ὁ ἀνὴρ ὁ λαλήσας πρὸς τὴν γυναῖκα.
You are the man * speaking with the woman.

λαλήσας is an aorist, active participle, nominative, singular, masculine (from λαλέω).

- ★ λαλήσας is adjectival. It modifies ὁ ἀνὴρ.
- ★ The case, number and gender of the participle match the case, number and gender of the noun being modified (ὁ ἀνὴρ).
- ★ The underlined words are the participial phrase.
- ★ IMPORTANT: The adjectival participle almost always has the article.

Substantival Participle

ὁ πιστεύσας καὶ βαπτισθεὶς σωθήσεται[1].
The believing and baptized will be saved.
= The (one who) believes and is baptized will be saved.

πιστεύσας is an aorist, active participle, nominative, singular, masculine.
βαπτισθεὶς is an aorist, passive participle, nominative, singular, masculine.

- ★ πιστεύσας and βαπτισθεὶς are substantival. They are the subject of the verb.
- ★ The case, number and gender match the implied subject. (The man[2] who believes and is baptized.)
- ★ The smoothed out version adds the implied subject. This is a legitimate translation.
- ★ IMPORTANT: The substantival participle almost always has the article.

---

[1] From σώζω. Notice the future passive clue (θησ).

[2] Often, the masculine form is gender inclusive, much in the same way as in older English "mankind" referred to all humanity, not just males.

Substance

By "substance" I mean the things. The people. The places. The "stuff" of life. The first thing a child does when she learns a language is point and name: "Mommy!" "Daddy!" "Bottle!"

The names are **nouns**. For example,

monkey.

If you want to call special attention to a thing you can use the **article**. Not just any monkey.

the monkey.

If you want to further describe what you see, you can attach an **adjective**.

The *brown* monkey.

If you get tired of saying monkey over and over, you use a **pronoun** to stand in for the noun.

I saw the brown monkey. *It* was eating bananas.

Motion

What if you want to describe how the things move? You would select a **verb**, an action word.

The monkey *flies*!

And if you want to further describe the action you use an **adverb** to modify the verb.

The monkey flies *joyfully*!

What if you wanted to use a verbal idea to modify a noun? You would have to create a verbal adjective. These are called **participles**. Don't let the scary word scare you. It's simple. As simple as...

a *flying* monkey

See? The participle "flying" is a verbal idea, used like an adjective to describe a noun — a verbal adjective. These are participles. Usually, in English, these are the "ing" words.

Infinitives are the "to be" verbs. They are verbal nouns.

To love is my highest ambition.

Do you see how "to love" in the sentence above could be replaced with a noun?

Health is my highest ambition.

The "to- _____" combination acts just like a noun, but not just any noun, a noun in motion. Infinitives are verbal nouns.

Relationship

What if you want to describe the relationships between things? You use a **preposition**.

The monkey flew *over* my house!

And if you want to link two words or ideas together you use **conjunctions**.

The monkey *and* his wife were laughing at how easy this is.

I want to teach you Greek but I do not want to bore you.

Don't let anyone fool you. At the core, language is simple. Substantives (nouns, articles, adjectives, pronouns) are put into Motion (verbs, adverbs, participles, infinitives). Relationships are described by prepositions and conjunctions.

Language is so simple that every one of God's children uses it. In fact, the stupidest people do the most talking.

Grammar only gets confusing when you get into the details. When you begin to feel overwhelmed in your study of Greek, review this basic summary. It will help you keep the big picture in mind.

2. The Greek Alphabet

Lesson in a Nutshell

The Greek Alphabet is similar to the English alphabet and may be learned using the following memory aids:

1. a, b, "g" d e ($\alpha \beta \gamma \delta \varepsilon$)
2. zeta ate a theta! ($\zeta \eta \theta$)
3. Line up i - u ($\iota \_ \kappa \lambda \mu \nu \xi o \pi \_ \rho \sigma \tau \upsilon$)
   1. drop "j" and "q" (which are junque anyway).
   2. add ξ. There is "no" reason for ξ to be between "n" and "o."
4. Poughkeepsie ($\varphi \chi \psi$) and ω.

Name	Upper Case	Lower Case	Pronunciation	Transliteration
Alpha	A	α	car	a
Beta	B	β	book	b
Gamma	Γ	γ	good	g
Delta	Δ	δ	donkey	d
Epsilon	E	ε	every	e
Zeta	Z	ζ	zebra	z
Eta	H	η	beta	ē
Theta	Θ	θ	think	th
Iota	I	ι	intrigue	i
Kappa	K	κ	kitchen	k
Lambda	Λ	λ	lazy	l
Mu	M	μ	monkey	m
Nu	N	ν	nut	n
Xi	Ξ	ξ	extra	x
Omicron	O	o	blot	o
Pi	Π	π	person	p
Rho	P	ρ	rotten	r

Name	Upper Case	Lower Case	Pronunciation	Transliteration
Sigma	Σ	σ, ς	snake	s
Tau	Τ	τ	trick	t
Upsilon	Υ	υ	super	u/y
Phi	Φ	φ	phone	ph
Chi	Χ	χ	Bach	ch
Psi	Ψ	ψ	psychology	ps
Omega	Ω	ω	no	ō

Alphabet Memorization Tricks

	1					2										3								4				
a	b	c	d	e	f̶	g̶	h̶	i	j̶	k	l	m	n	o	p	q̶	r	s	t	u	v̶	w̶	x̶	y̶	z̶
α	β	γ	δ	ε	ζ	η θ	ι		κ	λ	μ	ν ξ	o	π		ρ	σ ς	τ	υ	φ	χ	ψ	ω

a b "g" d e   zeta ate a theta!   there is "no" reason for ξ to be there!   write your own ending
(Poughkeepsie)

The Greek alphabet has much in common with the English alphabet. I find it easiest to memorize it in blocks.

The first five letters are as easy as a, b, "g," d, e.

1

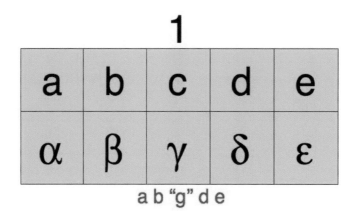

a b "g" d e

Just remember to replace the "c" in the English alphabet with a "g" (γ) in the Greek alphabet.

Next, we depart from the English script because something truly terrifying happens: In a horrifying act of alphabet cannibalism, "Zeta Ate-a Theta!"

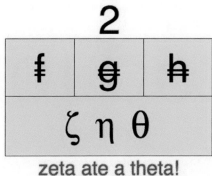

zeta ate a theta!

This is my corny trick to remember the letters zeta, eta, and theta.

Next comes a long stretch of thirteen letters that pretty much correspond to the English alphabet.

there is "**n o**" reason for ξ to be there!

First, let's get rid of the English letters "j" and "q." These are JunQue! After all,

- There is no soft "j" sound in Greek (as in "jelly").

- "Q" is a lame letter, don't you agree? It is codependent on a "u" just to survive. So throw it out!

Otherwise the letters line up nicely with the exception of ξ. ξ is inserted between "n" and "o." I remember this by reminding myself that there is "N-O" reason for ξ to be there!

One other little quirk is that there are two forms of sigma. One is used when the letter appears within a word and the other is used when it comes at the end, (called "final sigma"). The word κόσμος is a good example of this.

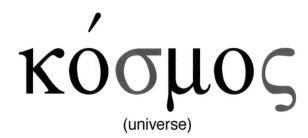

(universe)

That's all but the last four letters. At this point we depart again from the English alphabet and write our own ending.

Everyone knows that the last letter of the Greek alphabet is ω, right? So all we have to learn is the three letters φ, χ, and ψ.

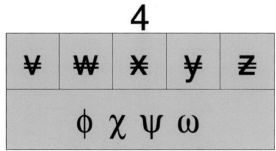

write your own ending
(Poughkeepsie, NY)

This is my weakest memory aid, but it helps me to think of the town of Poughkeepsie, New York. The consonants don't line up exactly with the Greek ones but it points me in the right direction.

Pough = φ phi

kee   = χ chi

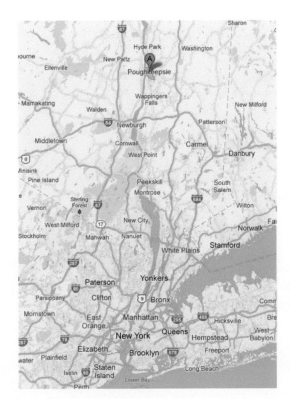

ρSie = Ψ psi

If that doesn't help you, maybe you can come up with a better way to remember the last four letters. Let me know and I'll make you famous.

One of the best ways to learn the Greek alphabet is to practice writing it as you say the names of the letters aloud. Open up the "Take a Hike" workbook and practice writing and saying the letters out loud.

3. Vowels & Diphthongs, Syllables, Punctuation

Lesson in a Nutshell

Greek vowels are very similar to English vowels: α (η), ε, ι, ο (ω), υ.

The diphthongs are αι (aisle), ει (eight), οι (oil), αυ (sauerkraut), ου (soup), υι (suite), ευ/ηυ (feud).

One syllable per vowel or diphthong.

Vowels

Greek vowels are similar to English vowels. I think of the η as a long "α" sound and the ω as a long "o" sound.

a	α	η
e	ε	
i	ι	
o	ο	ω
u	υ	

Diphthongs

Diphthongs are two vowels that combine to create a single sound. I find it helpful to remember the diphthongs like this:

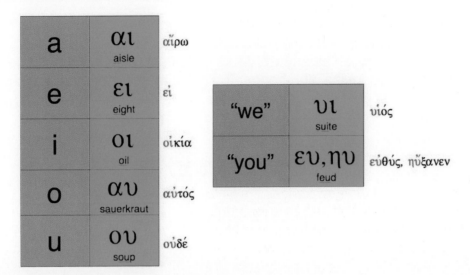

In most cases, the diphthongs make the sound you would expect if you were to say the two single vowels together very quickly.

Do diphthongs seem stupid to you? Think about English. We have diphthongs and they are not nearly as consistent.

Consider the words

eight
height
Leigh (girl's name)

Notice how inconsistent English is. Aren't you glad you are learning Greek instead of English?

Improper Diphthongs

Sometimes at the end of a word, you will notice that an iota has crawled under an α, η, or ω like this:

$$α \quad η \quad ω$$

These are called "improper diphthongs." The iota is not pronounced.

Syllables

To pronounce Greek, it is important to be able to divide Greek words into syllables. Thankfully, this is relatively easy — much easier than English. The rule is simple:

One syllable per vowel (or diphthong).

You can see how many syllables any word has by counting vowels/diphthongs. Notice how important it is to recognize diphthongs. If you fail to see them you will create two syllables where there should only be one. I underlined them and put them in bold type to help you see them.

ἄνθρωπος
man

ἄν-θρω-πος[1]

γίνομαι
I become

γί-νο-μαι

---

[1] You might wonder how to place the consonants. Actually, this is not important since when you put the word together and say it, it will sound the same whether you put the consonants with the preceding vowel or the one that follows. But in case you want to know, here are the rules:
- Single consonants and consonant clusters that can be pronounced together go with the following vowel.
- A consonant cluster that cannot be pronounced together is divided. The first part goes with the preceding vowel and the second part goes with the following vowel. You can tell if a consonant cluster can be pronounced together by two tests: 1. Try it! If it is awkward it probably does not belong together. For example, in ἄνθρωπος, try saying the letters νθρ together. Doesn't work, does it? 2. Look up the letters in a dictionary. If no words start with a given set of consonants, it is probably a cluster that cannot be pronounced together.
- Double letters are divided (see ἀλλά below).

But please do not sweat too much about this. The important thing is to recognize the vowels, not to be precise in the division of consonants.

Notice the difference between διά and καί in the next two examples. Since ια in διά is not a diphthong, it is separated into two syllables. But since the αι in καί is a diphthong, this word remains a single syllable.

διά
through
δι-ά

καί
and
καί

ἐγώ
I
ἐ-γώ

εἰμί
I am
εἰ-μί

ἔρχομαι
I come or go
ἔρ-χο-μαι

λέγω
I say
λέ-γω

ποιέω
I make or do
ποι-έ-ω

ἀδελφός
brother
ἀ-δελ-φός

ἀλλά
nevertheless
ἀλ-λά

ἀπό
from
ἀ-πό

Practice dividing some words into syllables in the "Take a Hike" workbook.

Punctuation

Greek punctuation is super easy:

- The period and comma in Greek are identical to English.
- The Greek question mark looks like an English semicolon.
- The Greek semicolon looks like a dot above the line.

Greek	English
.	.
,	,
;	?
·	;

4. Pronunciation, Breathing Marks, Accents

Lesson in a Nutshell

The first sound of a letter is the sound that it makes.

There are three accents (´ ` ˆ). Stress the syllable with the accent.

Every word that starts with a vowel will have a breathing mark. The smooth breathing (᾽) is not pronounced. The rough breathing (῾) sounds like an "h."

Pronunciation

The pronunciation of Greek is marvelously consistent.

For starters, if you know how to say the name of a letter, you know the sound it makes since the first sound of the letter's name is the sound of the letter.

For example, Beta makes a "b" sound. Delta makes a "d" sound.

As we have seen, every vowel or diphthong in Greek gets its own syllable. This can create words with a large number of syllables. For example, take θεάομαι, which means "I behold." It would be broken up as follows:

$$θε – ά – ο – μαι$$
(αι is a diphthong, remember)

It would be pronounced like this.

$$thē - \mathbf{a} - o - mai$$

The best way to learn pronunciation is not to read about how to do it, but to hear it and practice.

Please spend plenty of time with the pronunciation video.

Also, be sure to speak words OUT LOUD as you study Greek. Your friends may think you are losing your mind but it will significantly speed your learning.

Breathing Marks

Every Greek word that begins with a vowel (or diphthong) will have a breathing mark over it.

There are two breathing marks, rough and smooth.

smooth	rough
᾿	῾
silent (not pronounced)	pronounced like an "h"

For example, the word ἀνήρ (male/husband) is pronounced "**a-nēr**." It has a smooth breathing mark which is not pronounced.

The word ἁμαρτία (sin) is pronounced "**ha-mar-ti-a**." Notice that it has a rough breathing mark which is pronounced like an "h" at the beginning of the word.

Accents

Almost every Greek word will have an accent over one of the syllables. Originally, these were pitch accents which either rose, fell, or went up and down.

Accent	Name	Original Sound
´	acute	rising
`	grave	falling
⌒	circumflex	rising then falling

Today, most people just place stress on the syllable with the accent. There is debate about the importance of learning the rules of accenting. Since these can get rather complicated and we only have to read Greek, not write it, we will not worry about learning the rules of accenting right now.

Instead, when we read a Greek word, <u>we will stress the syllable which has the accent</u>.

There is one additional accent that you will run across now and then. It is called a *diaeresis. (dee-AR-e-sis)* It looks like this:

··

An example of the diaeresis can be found in the word "Isaiah."

'Ησαΐας
(Isaiah)

Whatever vowel the diaeresis stands above is pronounced as a separate syllable.

Normally the diphthong αι would function as a single syllable, like this:

'Ησ – αί – ας

But since the iota has a diaeresis above it, the alpha and the iota each are pronounced separately, like this:

'Ησ – α – ΐ – ας

You will not see many of these.

The Crossroads

Conjunctions and Prepositions

5. Conjunctions

Lesson in a Nutshell

Conjunctions connect words and phrases and clauses. They do not change form.

Conjunctions are used to connect words, phrases and clauses. They are very common. Thankfully, they do not change form. Here is a list of common conjunctions. (The number is how many times they occur in the New Testament.)

Conjunctions		
ἀλλά	638	but, yet, rather, nevertheless
γάρ	1041	for, so, then
δέ	2792	but, and, rather, now, then
ἐάν	351	if, when
εἰ	502	if, that, whether
ἕως	146	until, while
ἤ	343	or, either, nor, what, than
ἵνα	663	in order that, that, so that
καθώς	182	as, just as, even as
καί	9161	and, even, also, but, yet
ὅταν	123	whenever, when
ὅτι	1296	that, so that, because, for
οὐδέ	143	and not, neither, nor
οὖν	499	so, therefore, consequently
οὕτως	208	in this manner, thus, so
σύν	128	with, together with
τέ	215	and, and so, so
τότε	160	then, therefore
ὡς	504	as, like, because, when, while

There is nothing odd about Greek conjunctions. They behave very much like English conjunctions.

Just in Case You Are Curious

Question: What is the difference between a phrase and a clause?
Answer: Clauses contain a subject doing the action of a verb. Phrases do not.

Examples of Phrases

- through the looking glass
- happily, and without reservation
- over the rainbow
- because of the large explosion

Notice that in every case there is no subject and the thoughts are incomplete.

Examples of Clauses

- bald *is* beautiful
- I *was happy* to finish my work
- might does not always *make* right
- although he *was silent*
- whenever she *loses* her patience
- when the saints *go* marching in

In each of these clauses, there is a subject doing the action of a *verb.*

Clauses may be divided into two types: independent and dependent.

Independent clauses can stand on their own as complete sentences if they want to. The clauses in black print are independent clauses. Add punctuation and they make complete sentences.

Bald *is* beautiful.
I *was happy* to finish my work.
Might does not always *make* right.

The clauses in red print are dependent clauses. They must be attached to a sentence to make sense. For example:

Although he was silent, it was clear that he was angry.
The veins in her head get big whenever she *loses* her patience.
I want to be in that number when the saints *go* marching in.

6. Prepositions

Lesson in a Nutshell

> Prepositions place one thing relative to another thing. They do not change form. The meaning of the preposition can vary, depending on the case of its object. Greek prepositions are very flexible in meaning.

Prepositions are the little words that place things relative to other things. As I like to say, they are everything you can do with a box.

You can be <u>in the box</u>
You can walk <u>around the box</u>
You can slide <u>through the box</u>
You can sit <u>under the box</u>
You fly <u>over the box</u>
Etc. Etc.

Prepositions normally stand at the head of prepositional phrases (the underlined words above).

The chart below summarizes the meanings of the most common Greek prepositions. (The bold entries are the spatial ideas.)

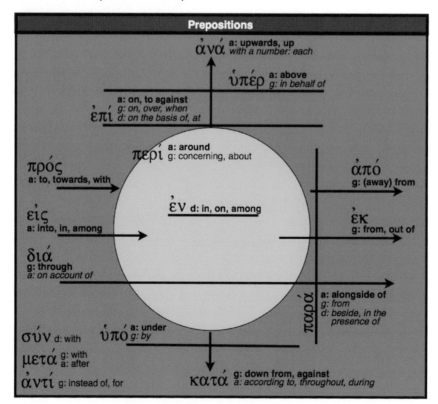

Greek prepositions have had an enormous impact on English vocabulary. Paying attention to this may help you to remember them. Here are some examples.

Greek Word	English Cognate
ἐν	inside
διά δι᾽	diagnosis
παρά παρ᾽	parallel
εἰς	eisegesis
περί	pericardial
ἐκ ἐξ	extravert
ἀντί	antigravity
ὑπέρ	hyperbole
ἐπί ἐπ᾽ ἐφ᾽	epicenter
ἀπό	apostasy

One Oddity of Greek Prepositions

The only trick of the Greek preposition is that the meaning of the preposition changes depending on the case of its object. This is nothing like English, so it will take a little effort to grasp. We will explain this when we study nouns. **Do not worry about it** until we get there.

Here is a chart to illustrate how the case of the preposition's object changes its meaning.

Preposition	Object	Translation
μετά	τούτων (genitive case)	**with** these
μετά	ταῦτα (accusative case)	**after** these
παρά	ἀνθρωπον (accusative case)	**alongside of** a man
παρά	ἀνθρωπου (genitive case)	**from** a man
παρά	ἀνθρωπῳ (dative case)	**beside** a man

Preposition	Object	Translation
διά	τούτων (genitive case)	**through** these
διά	ταῦτα (accusative case)	**on account of** these

Greek prepositions are very fluid. At the risk of overwhelming you, on the next two pages is a chart of the full range of meaning of most of the Greek prepositions. Do not worry about memorizing it! Just be aware of the flexibility of the preposition.

Preposition	used with	Usage	Translation
ἀνά	A	Distributive Spatial	*in the midst of* *up, motion upward* (with verbs)
ἀπό	G	Separation Source Cause Partitive Agency	*away from* *from, out of* *because of* *of* *by, from* (rare)
δία	G	Agency Means Spatial Temporal	*by, through* *through* *through* *through(out), during*
	A	Cause Spatial	*because of, on account of, for the sake of* *through* (rare)
εἰς	A	Spatial Temporal Purpose Result Reference/Respect Advantage Disadvantage In place of ἐν	*into, toward, in* *for, throughout* *for, in order to, to* *so that, with the result that* *with respect to, with reference to* *for* *against* (with various nuances)
ἐκ	G	Source Separation Temporal Cause Partitive Means	*out of, from* *away from, from* *from, from [this point]...on* *because of* *of* *by, from*
ἐν	D	Spatial/Sphere Temporal Association Cause Instrumental Reference/Respect Manner Thing Possessed Standard (Dative of Rule) equivalent to εἰς	*in* *in, within, when, while, during* *with* (often close personal relationship) *because of* *by, with* *with respect to / with reference to* *with* *with* (in the sense of which possesses) *according to the standard of* (with verbs of motion)
ἐπί	G	Spatial Temporal Cause	*on, upon, at, near* *in the time of, during* *on the basis of*
	D	Spatial Temporal Cause	*on, upon, against, at, near* *at, at the time of, during* *on the basis of*
	A	Spatial Temporal	*on, upon, to, up to, against* *for, over a period of*

		Spatial	down from, throughout
κατά	G	Opposition	against
		Source	from
	A	Standard	in accordance with, corresponding to
		Spatial	along, through (extension); toward, up to (direction)
		Temporal	at, during
		Distributive	indicating the division of a greater whole into individual parts
		Purpose	for the purpose of
		Reference/Respect	with respect to, with reference to
μετά	G	Association/Accompaniment	with, in company with
		Spatial	with, among
		Manner	with (attendant circumstance)
	A	Temporal	after, behind
		Spatial	after, behind (rare)
παρά	G	Source	from
		Agency	from, by
	D	Spatial	near, beside
		Sphere	in the sight of, before (someone)
		Association (= simple dative)	with (someone/something)
	A	Spatial	by, alongside of, near, on
		Comparison	in comparison to, more than
		Opposition	against, contrary to
περί	G	Reference	concerning
		Advantage / Representation	on behalf of, for (=ὑπέρ)
	A	Spatial	around, near
		Temporal	about, near
		Reference/Respect	with regard/reference to
πρό	G	Spatial	before, in front of, at
		Temporal	before
		Rank/Priority	before
πρός	A	Purpose	for, for the purpose of
		Spatial	toward
		Temporal	toward, for (duration)
		Result	so that, with the result that
		Opposition	against
		Association	with, in company with
σύν	D	Accompaniment/Association	with, in association (company) with
ὑπέρ	G	Representation/Advantage	on behalf of, for the sake of
		Reference/Respect	concerning, with reference to (=περί)
		Substitution	in place of, instead of (=ἀντί)
	A	Spatial	over, above
		Comparison	more than, beyond
ὑπό	G	(Ultimate) Agency	by
		Intermediate Agency	through (with active verbs)
		Means	by (rare)
	A	Spatial	under, below
		Subordination	under (the rule of)

Noun Rest

7. Nouns
(case, number & gender)

Lesson in a Nutshell

English nouns usually change form to tell you their number (singular or plural).

Greek nouns have:

a. case (nominative, genitive, dative, accusative). The case tells you the function the word performs in the sentence. In English this is accomplished by word order.

Case	Meaning	Keywords
Nominative	Subject of the sentence	
Genitive	Possession	of
Dative	Indirect object	in, with to, by
Accusative	Direct object	

b. number (singular and plural) and

c. gender (masculine or feminine or neuter).

Before you read on, let me beg you not to panic. What you learn in this section will apply to all substantives. When you grasp these concepts you will be well on your way to understanding Greek.

Also, don't forget that we will be encountering these ideas in a much more interesting way — in the Greek text itself. So if you read this and it confuses you, don't worry. It will become clearer as we go along.

Noun Syntax

As we have said, nouns are verbal tags we put on the various pieces of our world.

Wall
Woman
Man
Subway
Car
Dog
Cat
etc. etc.

Nouns describe the stuff of the universe. There is a lot of stuff so there are a lot of nouns. As Steve Martin once complained about the French language, "Those French have a different word for everything!" Exactly. Every language has a different <u>word</u> for every <u>thing</u>.

Greek nouns and other substantives have <u>case</u>, <u>number</u>, and <u>gender</u>. The easiest way to get at these ideas is to begin with English. We will begin with number, since English and Greek number are the same.

Number

Consider two variations of the same noun:

cat
cats

What is the difference between the two? In both cases we are describing a cute, furry critter, right?

The difference is in the **number**. "Cat" is singular — it describes <u>one</u> cute, furry critter. "Cats" is plural — it describes two or more.

English nouns change form to tell us whether we are talking about one (singular) or more than one (plural).

Normally, in English, we add an "s" to the end of a word to make it plural.

cat (one)
cat<u>s</u> (two or more)

Nice and simple, right?

Sometimes English does other things. Consider these two words.

man (singular)
men (plural)

Why not just say "man<u>s</u>" if we want the plural form of "man?" Because no language is perfectly consistent. In this case, the number was changed by altering the vowel in the middle of the word.

And there are even some words that use the same form in the singular and plural:

deer (singular)
deer (plural)

If you are tempted to gripe about Greek, remember that English is at least as crazy!

Gender

Consider these three nouns:

Prince

Princess

Monarch

What is the difference? They all define someone lucky enough to be royalty, right?

The difference between these three lucky people is their **gender**. These nouns are by nature either masculine (prince), or feminine (princess) or neuter/undefined (monarch).

The "gender" of a noun tells us whether it is masculine, feminine or neuter.

Greek gender is much like English gender, but there is one big difference:

In English, most nouns are not gender specific. You might think of English nouns as following a "don't ask, don't tell" policy. They simply don't declare their gender.

Consider the following nouns:

Lamp

Bee

Tree

Sky

You would not refer to any of these nouns as "he" or "she." You would refer to all of them as "it." It isn't that they are neuter. It's just that the noun doesn't tell us the gender so we declare it neuter by default.

A few English nouns have a trace of gender. For example, we might call the church or a ship "she," but most English nouns are genderless.

Here is an important difference between Greek and English

*Every Greek noun, without exception, is
either masculine or feminine or neuter.*

In some cases the gender is logical to us (called natural gender).

"man" (ἄνθρωπος) is a male noun.

"woman" (γύνη) is a feminine noun.

But in most cases, we can discern no rhyme or reason to it.

"word" (λόγος) is a masculine noun.

"sin" (ἁμαρτια) is a feminine noun.

"book" (βίβλιον) is a neuter noun.

You must get used to the idea that <u>every</u> Greek noun, without exception, will be either masculine or feminine or neuter.

Case

The concepts of number and gender are fairly easy. You may find it harder to grasp the idea of case. Don't worry. We will have plenty of time to let this sink in. And when you comprehend Greek case, it will do wonders for your English as well as your Greek grammar.

Venture on!

Consider two different variations of the same word:

I
Me

Unless you have a serious mental disorder, you consider "I" and "me" to be the same person. I am me, right? If "I" am not "me" I need to see a shrink, pronto!

<u>So here's the big question</u>: Why do we need two words to describe I/me?

<u>Here's the big answer</u>: Because the two forms tell us how the word functions in a sentence. This is the **case** of the noun.

That is so important that I will say it again in red:

Because the two forms tell us how the word **functions in the sentence.**
This is the **case** of the noun.

And in orange:

Because the two forms tell us how the word **functions in the sentence.**
This is the **case** of the noun.

Allow me to demonstrate. Which sentence sounds correct to you:

#1   I am going to the store.

#2   Me am going to the store.

Even if you can't explain why, you will identify sentence #1 as correct. It just sounds better. But why?

Because we use "I" when we want to identify ourselves as the subject — the one doing the action of the verb. "I" is called subjective case.

Now look at these two sentences:

#1   My wife punched I!

#2   My wife punched me!

Which of those two sentences sounds correct?

Hopefully you said the second: "My wife punched <u>me</u>!" sounds right to the English ear. But why?

Because we use "me" when we want to identify ourselves as the object — the one receiving the action of the verb. "Me" is called objective case.

We learn to make these shifts intuitively, just from listening to people talk, even if we cannot explain the grammar. If you are an English speaker, the logic of the following sentences is probably self-evident.

Me don't do things. I do things.

I do things to me. I don't do things to I.

You don't give things to I. You give them to me.

Do you see how "I' and "me" change form depending on whether they are giving or receiving the action of the verb?

"I" and "me" are examples of **case**.

What is case? Three more times to make sure you never forget:

Case is the **form** a word takes to tell us how it **functions in a sentence.**
Case is the **form** a word takes to tell us how it **functions in a sentence.**
Case is the **form** a word takes to tell us how it **functions in a sentence.**

Now strap on your seat belts for a loop-the-loop. Here is why English students find Greek baffling.

> *English nouns don't change form very much.*
>
> They rely instead on their
> <u>order in a sentence</u>
> to tell us what role they play.
>
> *Greek nouns change form like crazy.*
>
> They <u>change form</u>
> to tell us what role
> they play in the sentence.

As we get into the Greek text we will see examples and this will become clearer. But to get us started, consider an example. Here are two very different events:

The dog is biting the man.

The man is biting the dog.

Notice that the words "man" and "dog" do not change form at all. How do we know who is biting whom?

By the word order.

English puts the subject before the verb and the object after it. But Greek doesn't depend on word order to tell us what role each word is playing in a sentence.

In Greek, these two sentences mean the same thing.

ὁ κυων δακνει τον ανθρωπον.
The dog is biting the man.

τον ανθρωπον δακνει ὁ κυων.
The man ← is biting←the dog.

The translation of both of these sentences is

"The dog is biting the man."

HUH??

It looks like the dog is doing the biting in the first sentence but in the second sentence it looks to an English speaker as if the man is the one doing the biting. We assume this because of the word order.

In the second sentence, "the man" comes before the verb so we assume he is doing the biting.

But Greek tells the subject by changing the form of the word, not by putting it before the verb.

I highlighted the ways the Greek nouns changed in red. Don't worry that you can't recognize these changes yet. You will soon.

One More Time

English nouns don't change form very much.

They rely instead on their
order in a sentence
to tell us what role they play.

But Greek nouns change form like crazy.

They change form
to tell us what role
they play in the sentence.

The good news is that the patterns of change are consistent and easy to spot. In many ways, Greek is easier than English. Once you learn the patterns, it's a piece of cake.

Remember:

Case is the **form** a word takes to tell us how it **functions in a sentence.**
Case is the **form** a word takes to tell us how it **functions in a sentence.**
Case is the **form** a word takes to tell us how it **functions in a sentence.**

There are four[1] primary cases in Greek that correspond with the four main roles the nouns play in the sentence: [2]

1. Nominative (subject)
2. Genitive (possession)
3. Dative (indirect object)
4. Accusative (object)

Nominative Case (Subject)

If a noun is in the nominative case it serves as the subject of the sentence.

ὁ ἄνθρωπος γράφει.
The   man   is writing.

"The man" is in the nominative case since it is the subject of the sentence.

Accusative Case (Object)

If a noun is in the accusative case, it serves as the direct object of the verb.

ὁ ἄνθρωπος γράφει τὴν ἐπίστολην.
The   man is writing the   letter.

---

[1] The fifth case is the vocative case. It is used for direct address, as in the prayer, "Lord, grant us peace." "Lord," in this example, would be in the vocative case. The vocative case is not very common and it is easy to spot from the context so we will not worry about it right now.

[2] As we become more skilled at Greek we will see that there are many more possibilities than are listed here, especially in the genitive and dative case. This is just to get us started.

Dative Case (Indirect Object)

If a noun is in the dative case it identifies it as the indirect object.

ὁ ανθρωπος γραφει την ἐπιστολην τη εκκλησια.
The   man   is writing   the   letter   to the   church.

I think of it as a ricochet. The subject (nominative case) initiates the action which is directed at the direct object (accusative case). The action bounces off the direct object and hits the indirect object (dative case).

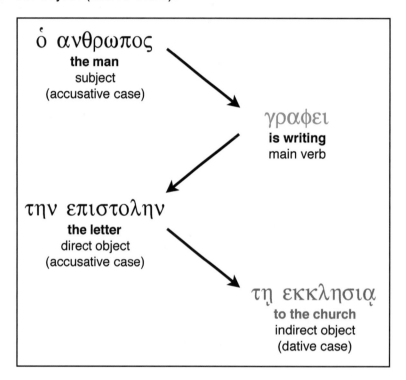

Language is much more nuanced than the ricochet of a bullet. Here are some other examples.

To get started, we will use the following prepositions with the dative.

"to" "in" "with" "by"

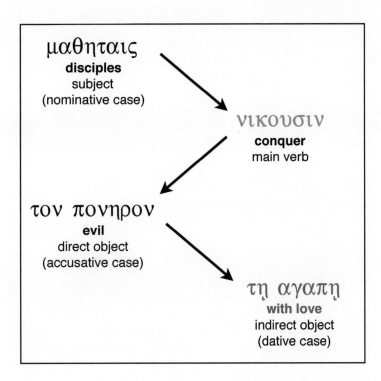

οἱ αποστολοι
the apostles
subject
(nominative case)

λεγουσιν
are speaking
main verb

την αληθεια
the truth
direct object
(accusative case)

τη συναγωγη
in the synagogue
indirect object
(dative case)

μαθηταις
disciples
subject
(nominative case)

νικουσιν
conquer
main verb

τον πονηρον
evil
direct object
(accusative case)

τη αγαπη
with love
indirect object
(dative case)

As we progress we will find that the dative is capable of a much larger range of meaning than this.

Genitive Case (Possession)

If a noun is in the genitive case it shows possession.

$$\overset{\text{`}}{\text{ο}} \ \lambda ο γ ο ς \ \ θ ε ο υ$$
the   word   of God
(= God's Word)

We will use the keyword

"of"

with the genitive case.

The keyword "of" is just to get us off the runway. The genitive is capable of great feats. It can do much more than show possession. We will explore this when we get into the Greek text.

Don't Forget The Big Picture

Case is the **form** a word takes to tell us how it **functions in a sentence.**
Case is the **form** a word takes to tell us how it **functions in a sentence.**
Case is the **form** a word takes to tell us how it **functions in a sentence.**

And

English nouns don't change form very much.

They rely instead on their
<u>order in a sentence</u>
to tell us what role they play.

But Greek nouns change form like crazy.

They <u>change form</u>
to tell us what role
they play in the sentence.

Here is a summary of the four primary Greek cases.

Case	Meaning	Keywords
Nominative	Subject of the sentence	
Genitive	Possession	of
Dative	Indirect object	in, with, to, by
Accusative	Direct object	

Remember: every noun will have:

Case (which tells us how it functions in the sentence)
Number (which tells us if it is singular or plural)
Gender (which tells us if it is masculine, feminine or neuter.)

The possible variations of case, number and gender are as follows:

Case	Number	Gender
Nominative **G**enitive **D**ative **A**ccusative	**S**ingular **P**lural	**M**asculine **F**eminine **N**euter

The main differences between Greek and English are summarized in the chart below.

Comparison of Greek and English

	Case	Number	Gender
English	depends on word order	much like Greek	only a few nouns declare their gender
Greek	depends on morphology (changed forms)	much like English	all nouns declare their gender

That's it for noun syntax. On to noun morphology!

8. First Declension

Lesson in a Nutshell

First declension nouns are usually feminine and end in an α or η

Every Greek noun will give us three pieces of information about itself:

1. Its case tells us the role it plays in the sentence.
2. Its number tells us whether it is singular or plural.
3. Its gender tells us whether it is masculine, feminine, or neuter.

Case	Number	Gender
Nominative **G**enitive **D**ative **A**ccusative	**S**ingular **P**lural	**M**asculine **F**eminine **N**euter

But how will a given noun give us this information?

by inflection

"Inflection" is just a fancy word for "change." The words will change form ("morph") to give us the information. English words inflect a little bit. But Greek words inflect like crazy!

These inflections give us grammatical information about the word. It is nearly impossible to understand Greek without understanding grammar. But this is a good thing! Because once you know Greek, you will be a grammar whiz.

Greek nouns follow three patterns of inflection (change). These three patterns are called "declensions."

When you hear the word "declension"

think

"the pattern of change a noun follows to show me its case, number and gender."

On the second page of the Master Chart, locate the Noun Endings Chart.

Noun Endings

		Masculine (2nd declension)		Feminine (1st declension)		Neuter (2nd declension)		Masc / Fem (3rd declension)		Neuter (3rd declension)	
Singular	**Nominative** subject	ος	λογος word	α or η	αρχη beginning	ον	εργον work	ς	σαρξ flesh	—	φως light
	Genitive possession	ου	λογου of a word	ας or ης	αρχης of a beginning	ου	εργου of work	ος	σαρκος of flesh	ος	φωτος of light
	Dative in, with, to, by	ω	λογω to a word	α or η	αρχη to a beginning	ω	εργω to work	ι	σαρκι to flesh	ι	φωτι to light
	Accusative object	ον	λογον word	αν or ην	αρχην beginning	ον	εργον work	α	σαρκα flesh	—	φως light
Plural	**Nominative** subject	οι	λογοι words	αι	αρχαι beginnings	α	εργα works	ες	σαρκες fleshes	α	φωτα lights
	Genitive possession	ων	λογων of words	ων	αρχων of beginnings	ων	εργων of works	ων	σαρκων of fleshes	ων	φωτων of lights
	Dative in, with, to, by	οις	λογοις to words	αις	αρχαις to beginnings	οις	εργοις to works	σιν	σαρξιν to fleshes	σιν	φωσιν to lights
	Accusative object	ους	λογους words	ας	αρχας beginnings	α	εργα works	ας	σαρκας fleshes	α	φωτα lights

Notice that there are three declensions.

First declension nouns
(in blue)

are usually feminine

and their stem

usually ends in an α or an η.

Second declension nouns
(in blue)

are usually masculine or neuter

and their stem

usually ends in an ο.

		Masculine (2nd declension)		Feminine (1st declension)		Neuter (2nd declension)		Masc / Fem (3rd declension)		Neuter (3rd declension)	
Noun Endings												
Singular	Nominative subject	ος	λογος word	α or η	αρχη beginning	ον	εργον work	ς	σαρξ flesh	–	φως light
	Genitive possession	ου	λογου of a word	ας or ης	αρχης of a beginning	ου	εργου of work	ος	σαρκος of flesh	ος	φωτος of light
	Dative in, with, to, by	ω	λογω to a word	ᾳ or η	αρχη to a beginning	ω	εργω to work	ι	σαρκι to flesh	ι	φωτι to light
	Accusative object	ον	λογον word	αν or ην	αρχην beginning	ον	εργον work	α	σαρκα flesh	–	φως light
Plural	Nominative subject	οι	λογοι words	αι	αρχαι beginnings	α	εργα works	ες	σαρκες fleshes	α	φωτα lights
	Genitive possession	ων	λογων of words	ων	αρχων of beginnings	ων	εργων of works	ων	σαρκων of fleshes	ων	φωτων of lights
	Dative in, with, to, by	οις	λογοις to words	αις	αρχαις to beginnings	οις	εργοις to works	σιν	σαρξιν to fleshes	σιν	φωσιν to lights
	Accusative object	ους	λογους words	ας	αρχας beginnings	α	εργα works	ας	σαρκας fleshes	α	φωτα lights

Third declension nouns
(in yellow)

may be masculine, feminine, or neuter

and their stem

ends in a consonant.

This will become clearer as we go, so if you are a bit confused at this point do not worry!

Let's start by looking at a first declension noun: ἀρχή

1st Declension Endings		Feminine (1st declension)	
Singular	Nominative subject	α or η	αρχη beginning
	Genitive possession	ας or ης	αρχης of a beginning
	Dative in, with, to, by	ᾳ or η	αρχη to a beginning
	Accusative object	αν or ην	αρχην beginning
Plural	Nominative subject	αι	αρχαι beginnings
	Genitive possession	ων	αρχων of beginnings
	Dative in, with, to, by	αις	αρχαις to beginnings
	Accusative object	ας	αρχας beginnings

Look carefully at the table above. Notice how the endings change to tell us their case, number and gender.

There are eight forms of every noun. This makes sense.

four cases   X   two numbers = 8 forms

In the chart above, notice that in English translations there are only two forms of the word: "beginning" and "beginnings." This is because English does not inflect (change form) to tell us its case. It only changes to tell us if it singular or plural. English compensates for this by using word order and little helping words. English is not nearly as elegant as Greek!

Here are three more examples of first declension nouns: ὥρα, γραφή and δόξα. Notice how the endings are "tacked on" to the nouns. Also, notice how consistent the endings are.

You might notice that in the case of δόξα there is a shift between α and η. This is called an alpha-eta shift. Don't let it bother you. Just realize that in the first declension singular, the endings may be made with alphas or etas.

1st Declension Endings

		Feminine (1st declension)	
Singular	**Nominative** subject	α..η	ὥρα hour
	Genitive possession	ας..ης	ὥρας of an hour
	Dative in, with, to, by	ᾳ..η	ὥρᾳ to an hour
	Accusative object	αν..ην	ὥραν hour
Plural	**Nominative** subject	αι	ὧραι hours
	Genitive possession	ων	ὡρῶν of hours
	Dative in, with, to, by	αις	ὥραις to hours
	Accusative object	ας	ὥρας hours

1st Declension Endings

		Feminine (1st declension)	
Singular	**Nominative** subject	α..η	γραφή book
	Genitive possession	ας..ης	γραφῆς of a book
	Dative in, with, to, by	ᾳ..η	γραφῇ to a book
	Accusative object	αν..ην	γραφήν book
Plural	**Nominative** subject	αι	γραφαί books
	Genitive possession	ων	γραφῶν of books
	Dative in, with, to, by	αις	γραφαῖς to books
	Accusative object	ας	γραφάς books

1st Declension Endings

		Feminine (1st declension)	
Singular	**Nominative** subject	α..η	δόξα glory
	Genitive possession	ας..ης	δόξης of a glory
	Dative in, with, to, by	ᾳ..η	δόξῃ to a glory
	Accusative object	αν..ην	δόξαν glory
Plural	**Nominative** subject	αι	δόξαι glories
	Genitive possession	ων	δόξῶν of glories
	Dative in, with, to, by	αις	δόξαις to glories
	Accusative object	ας	δόξας glories

Here is an example of how the endings are used in a Greek sentence.

ἡ ζωή τῆς ἀλήθειας δίδωσιν δόξαν τῃ ψυχῇ
The life * of truth gives glory to the soul

word	ending	case	function in sentence
ζωή	ή	nominative	subject
ἀλήθειας	ας	genitive	possession
δόξαν	αν	accusative	object
ψυχῇ	ῇ	dative	indirect object

Here is another example in which the words are more mixed up (to us).

ζωὴν τῇ καρδίᾳ δίδωσιν ἡ ἀγάπη τῶν γραφῶν.
life   to the   heart   gives   the   love   *   of books.

word	ending	case	function in sentence
ζωὴν	ὴν	accusative	object
καρδίᾳ	ᾳ	dative	indirect object
ἀγάπη	η	nominative	subject
γραφῶν	ῶν	genitive	possession

I put this one out of normal English word order on purpose. Can you figure out how it would be translated?

The word "love" is in the nominative case, so it is the subject of the sentence.
The word "books" is in the genitive case so it indicates possession.
The word "life" is in the accusative case so it is the object of the verb.
The word ""heart" is in the dative case so it is the indirect object.

To translate this sentence into English we have to do two things:

1. We have to rearrange the words since English relies on word order to tell us what role each word plays in the sentence (case).

2. We have to add helping words ("of," "to").

So here it is:

The love of books gives life to the heart.

If you understand why this sentence is translated this way, you are well on your way to understanding how case works!

Use the "Take a Hike" Workbook to practice understanding Greek case.

Have fun!!

9. Second Declension

Lesson in a Nutshell

Second declension nouns are usually masculine or neuter and end in ο.

We saw that first declension nouns are generally end in α or η, were usually feminine and followed a single pattern.

The stem of second declension nouns generally end in an ο, may be masculine or neuter, and follow two patterns, which differ slightly from each other.

		Masculine (2nd declension)		Feminine (1st declension)		Neuter (2nd declension)		Masc / Fem (3rd declension)		Neuter (3rd declension)	
Singular	**Nominative** subject	ος	λογος word	α or η	αρχη beginning	ον	εργον work	ς	σαρξ flesh	—	φως light
	Genitive possession	ου	λογου of a word	ας or ης	αρχης of a beginning	ου	εργου of work	ος	σαρκος of flesh	ος	φωτος of light
	Dative in, with, to, by	ῳ	λογῳ to a word	ᾳ or η	αρχῃ to a beginning	ῳ	εργῳ to work	ι	σαρκι to flesh	ι	φωτι to light
	Accusative object	ον	λογον word	αν or ην	αρχην beginning	ον	εργον work	α	σαρκα flesh	—	φως light
Plural	**Nominative** subject	οι	λογοι words	αι	αρχαι beginnings	α	εργα works	ες	σαρκες fleshes	α	φωτα lights
	Genitive possession	ων	λογων of words	ων	αρχων of beginnings	ων	εργων of works	ων	σαρκων of fleshes	ων	φωτων of lights
	Dative in, with, to, by	οις	λογοις to words	αις	αρχαις to beginnings	οις	εργοις to works	σιν	σαρξιν to fleshes	σιν	φωσιν to lights
	Accusative object	ους	λογους words	ας	αρχας beginnings	α	εργα works	ας	σαρκας fleshes	α	φωτα lights

Noun Endings

Two Essential Things You Must Know About Every Noun

1. Its Gender

Every Greek noun will be <u>either</u> masculine <u>or</u> feminine <u>or</u> neuter.

2. Its Declension

Every Greek noun will be <u>either</u> first <u>or</u> second <u>or</u> third declension.

You do not know a Greek noun until you know its gender and declension, but once you know its gender and declension you know exactly what to expect in all of its eight forms.

Here are examples of two second declension, masculine nouns:

θεός and κόσμος.

Notice how the endings are "tacked on" to the words to show you the case, number, and gender.

Second Declension Masculine Noun			
		Masculine (2nd declension)	
Singular	**Nominative** subject	ος	θεός god
	Genitive possession	ου	θεοῦ of a god
	Dative in, with, to, by	ῳ	θεῷ to a god
	Accusative object	ον	θεόν god
Plural	**Nominative** subject	οι	θεοί gods
	Genitive possession	ων	θεῶν of gods
	Dative in, with, to, by	οις	θεοῖς to gods
	Accusative object	ους	θεούς gods

Second Declension Masculine Noun			
		Masculine (2nd declension)	
Singular	**Nominative** subject	ος	κόσμος world
	Genitive possession	ου	κόσμου of a world
	Dative in, with, to, by	ῳ	κόσμῳ to a world
	Accusative object	ον	κόσμον world
Plural	**Nominative** subject	οι	κόσμοι worlds
	Genitive possession	ων	κόσμων of worlds
	Dative in, with, to, by	οις	κόσμοις to worlds
	Accusative object	ους	κόσμους worlds

Here are examples of two second declension, neuter nouns:

εὐαγγέλιον and ἱερόν.

Notice again how the endings are "tacked on" to the words to show you the case, number, and gender.

Second Declension Neuter Noun			
		Neuter (2nd declension)	
Singular	**Nominative** subject	ον	ἱερόν temple
	Genitive possession	ου	ἱεροῦ of a temple
	Dative in, with, to, by	ῳ	ἱερῷ to a temple
	Accusative object	ον	ἱερόν temple
Plural	**Nominative** subject	α	ἱερά temples
	Genitive possession	ων	ἱερῶν of temples
	Dative in, with, to, by	οις	ἱεροῖς to gods
	Accusative object	α	ἱερά temples

Second Declension Neuter Noun			
		Neuter (2nd declension)	
Singular	**Nominative** subject	ον	εὐαγγέλιον gospel
	Genitive possession	ου	εὐαγγέλιου of a gospel
	Dative in, with, to, by	ῳ	εὐαγγέλιῳ to a gospel
	Accusative object	ον	εὐαγγέλιον gospel
Plural	**Nominative** subject	α	εὐαγγέλια gospels
	Genitive possession	ων	εὐαγγέλιων of gospels
	Dative in, with, to, by	οις	εὐαγγέλιοις to gospels
	Accusative object	α	εὐαγγέλια gospels

The patterns Greek nouns follow to show you case, number, and gender are marvelously consistent.

Savor the wonder!

Now observe how some second declension endings function in a Greek sentence.

ἄγγελος θεοῦ κηρύσσει εὐαγγέλιον ἀνθρώποις
(an)[1] angel   of God   announces   good news   to men.[2]

word	ending	case	function in sentence
ἄγγελος	ος	nominative	subject
θεοῦ	ου	genitive	possession
εὐαγγέλιον	ον	accusative	object
ἀνθρώποις	οις	dative	indirect object

The word order of the preceding sentence matched English word order exactly. Before you look at the answer, see if you can figure out how to translate the next sentence, which seems scrambled up.

---

[1] We will learn later, that there is no indefinite article ("a," "an") in Greek so we must supply it where it makes sense to do so.

[2] Greek uses the masculine gender to refer generally to all people.

νόμοις δουλοῦσιν τὸν κόσμον λόγοι ἀνθρώπων
to laws   (they) enslave   the   world   words   of men

word	ending	case	function in sentence
νόμοις	οις	dative	indirect object
κόσμον	ον	accusative	object
λόγοι	οι	nominative	subject
ἀνθρώπων	ων	genitive	possession

The word "words" is in the nominative case, so it is the subject of the sentence.
The word "men" is in the genitive case so it indicates possession.
The word "world" is in the accusative case so it is the object of the verb.
The word "laws" is in the dative case so it is the indirect object.

To translate this sentence into English we have to do two things:

1. We have to rearrange the words since English relies on word order to tell us what role each word plays in the sentence (case).

2. We have to add helping words ("of," "to").

So here it is:

Words of men enslave the world to laws.

Isn't Greek amazing?

Lexical Form of Nouns

How will you know if a noun is masculine, feminine or neuter? How will you know what declension it follows? You must learn all this when you learn the word.

A "lexicon" is a Greek dictionary. I'm not sure why we have to use fancy words. But most people call Greek dictionaries "lexicons."

"Lexical form" just refers to the way you will find it in the dictionary. Obviously, a Greek lexicon can't list every form of every word. It would be far too bulky. Instead, Greek lexicons list the word in its nominative singular form and tell you which pattern of inflection it follows.

Here is how this works:

If I were to look up the word λόγος (word) in the lexicon I would find it listed like this:

λόγος, ου, ὁ

What are the ου and the ὁ for?

ὁ is the masculine form of the article. It tells me that λόγος is a masculine noun.

The Article			
	M (2)	F (1)	N (2)
Nominative "the"	ὁ	ἡ	τό

The "ου" is the genitive ending of λόγος. It shows me which column to follow as λόγος goes through its eight changes.

Case Endings						
	Masculine (2nd declension)	**F**eminine (1st declension)	**N**euter (2nd declension)		**M**asc / **F**em (3rd declension)	**N**euter (3rd declension)
Nominative subject	ος — λογος word	α or η — αρχη beginning	ον — εργον work		ς — χειρ hand	— φως light
Genitive possession	ου — λογου of a word	ας or ης — αρχης of a beginning	ου — εργου of work		ος — χειρος of a hand	ος — φωτος of light
Dative in, with, to, by	ῳ — λογῳ to a word	ᾳ or ῃ — αρχῃ to a beginning	ῳ — εργῳ to work		ι — χειρι to a hand	ι — φωτι to light
Accusative object	ον — λογον word	αν or — αρχην beginning	ον — εργον work		α — χειρα hand	— φως light
Nominative subject	οι — λογοι words	αι — αρχαι beginnings	α — εργα works		ες — χειρες hands	α — φωτα lights
Genitive possession	ων — λογων of words	ων — αρχων of beginnings	ων — εργων of works		ω — χειρων of hands	ων — φωτων of lights
Dative in, with, to, by	οις — λογοις to words	αις — αρχαις to beginnings	οις — εργοις to works		σιν — χερσιν to hands	σιν — φωσιν to lights
Accusative object	ους — λογους words	ας — αρχας beginnings	α — εργα works		ας — χειρας hands	α — φωτα lights

The lexicon doesn't list all eight endings. That would be a long list!

λόγος, ου, ῳ, ον, οι, ων, οις, ους, ὁ

The lexicon assumes that if you know the genitive form, you will be able to supply the remaining endings. So "λόγος, ου, ὁ" gives you the information (in yellow above) and assumes you are smart enough to supply the rest of the column. You are, of course!

Now, let's look up ἀρχή in the lexicon. We find:

$$\text{ἀρχή, ῆς, ἡ}$$

ἡ is the feminine form of the article. It tells me that ἀρχή is a feminine noun.

The Article			
	M (2)	F (1)	N (2)
Nominative "the"	ὁ	ἡ	τό

ῆς is the genitive ending of ἀρχή. This shows me that I should follow the first declension.

Case Endings									
		Masculine (2nd declension)		**F**eminine (1st declension)		**N**euter (2nd declension)		**M**asc / **F**em (3rd declension)		**N**euter (3rd declension)
Nominative subject	ος	λογος word	α or η	αρχη beginning	ον	εργον work	ς	χειρ hand	—	φως light
Genitive possession	ου	λογου of a word	ας or ης	αρχης of a beginning	ου	εργου of work	ος	χειρος of a hand	ος	φωτος of light
Dative in, with, to, by	ῳ	λογῳ to a word	ᾳ or η	αρχη to a beginning	ῳ	εργῳ to work	ι	χειρι to a hand	ι	φωτι to light
Accusative object	ον	λογον word	αν or ην	αρχην beginning	ον	εργον work	α	χειρα hand	—	φως light
Nominative subject	οι	λογοι words	αι	αρχαι beginnings	α	εργα works	ες	χειρες hands	α	φωτα lights
Genitive possession	ων	λογων of words	ων	αρχων of beginnings	ων	εργων of works	ω	χειρων of hands	ων	φωτων of lights
Dative in, with, to, by	οις	λογοις to words	αις	αρχαις to beginnings	οις	εργοις to works	σιν	χερσιν to hands	σιν	φωσιν to lights
Accusative object	ους	λογους words	ας	αρχας beginnings	α	εργα works	α	χειρας hands	α	φωτα lights

Once again, the lexicon does not give me all eight endings.

$$\text{ἀρχή, ης, η, ην, αι, ων, αις, ας, ἡ}$$

The lexicon gives me the gender and the genitive form (in yellow above). I use my chart to figure out the rest. Soon I won't need a chart because I will remember this simple and consistent pattern.

Now, let's look up ἔργον in the lexicon. We find:

$$\text{ἔργον, ου, τό}$$

τό is the neuter form of the article. It tells me this is a neuter noun.

The Article		M (2)	F (1)	N (2)
Nominative "the"		ὁ	ἡ	τό

ου tells me that I should follow the second declension.

		Masculine (2nd declension)		**F**eminine (1st declension)		**N**euter (2nd declension)		**M**asc / **F**em (3rd declension)		**N**euter (3rd declension)	
Nominative subject		ος	λογος word	α or η	αρχη beginning	ον	εργον work	ς	χειρ hand	—	φως light
Genitive possession		ου	λογου of a word	ας or ης	αρχης of a beginning	ου	εργου of work	ος	χειρος of a hand	ος	φωτος of light
Dative in, with, to, by		ω	λογω to a word	α or η	αρχη to a beginning	ω	εργω to work	ι	χειρι to a hand	ι	φωτι to light
Accusative object		ον	λογον word	αν or ην	αρχην beginning	ον	εργον work	α	χειρα hand	—	φως light
Nominative subject		οι	λογοι words	αι	αρχαι beginnings	α	εργα works	ες	χειρες hands	α	φωτα lights
Genitive possession		ων	λογων of words	ων	αρχων of beginnings	ων	εργων of works	ω	χειρων of hands	ων	φωτων of lights
Dative in, with, to, by		οις	λογοις to words	αις	αρχαις to beginnings	οις	εργοις to works	σι ν	χερσιν to hands	σιν	φωσιν to lights
Accusative object		ους	λογου ς words	ας	αρχας beginnings	α	εργα works	α	χειρας hands	α	φωτα lights

By listing the article and the genitive form, the lexicon makes it possible to know every noun in every form.

10. Third Declension

Lesson in a Nutshell

Third declension nouns may be masculine, feminine, or neuter and have a stem that ends in a consonant.

First declension nouns are generally end in α or η, are usually feminine, and follow only one pattern.

Second declension nouns generally end in an o, may be masculine or neuter, and follow two patterns which differ slightly from each other.

Third declension nouns end in a consonant and may be masculine, feminine, or neuter. They are in yellow below.

		Masculine (2nd declension)		**Feminine** (1st declension)		**Neuter** (2nd declension)		**Masc / Fem** (3rd declension)		**Neuter** (3rd declension)	
Singular	**Nominative** subject	ος	λογος word	α or η	αρχη beginning	ον	εργον work	ς	σαρξ flesh	—	φως light
	Genitive possession	ου	λογου of a word	ας or ης	αρχης of a beginning	ου	εργου of work	ος	σαρκος of flesh	ος	φωτος of light
	Dative in, with, to, by	ῳ	λογῳ to a word	ᾳ or η	αρχη to a beginning	ῳ	εργῳ to work	ι	σαρκι to flesh	ι	φωτι to light
	Accusative object	ον	λογον word	αν or ην	αρχην beginning	ον	εργον work	α	σαρκα flesh	—	φως light
Plural	**Nominative** subject	οι	λογοι words	αι	αρχαι beginnings	α	εργα works	ες	σαρκες fleshes	α	φωτα lights
	Genitive possession	ων	λογων of words	ων	αρχων of beginnings	ων	εργων of works	ων	σαρκων of fleshes	ων	φωτων of lights
	Dative in, with, to, by	οις	λογοις to words	αις	αρχαις to beginnings	οις	εργοις to works	σιν	σαρξιν to fleshes	σιν	φωσιν to lights
	Accusative object	ους	λογους words	ας	αρχας beginnings	α	εργα works	ας	σαρκας fleshes	α	φωτα lights

Let's look first at the noun σάρξ. Σάρξ is a third declension, feminine noun. The stem of σάρξ is σαρκ. It is pretty easy to see how the endings are attached to σαρκ except in the nominative singular.

We would expect σαρκ̲ς̲

But instead we get σαρξ

Here is what happened: The κσ was changed to a ξ. If you think about it, this makes perfect sense. The sound a ξ makes is "κσ."

$$\sigma\alpha\rho\underline{\kappa\varsigma} \quad \rightarrow \quad \sigma\alpha\rho\underline{\xi}$$

Time Out

This the perfect opportunity to introduce you to the Square of Stops.

The Square of Stops is a table that tells you what happens when certain consonants collide. You can find it on page 6 of the Master Chart

Collision of Consonants
The Square of Stops

The Square of Stops is a nifty way to show how consonants collide to create new letters. For the most part, it is intuitive.

Square of Stops				
	unvoiced	voiced	aspirate	+ σ	+ θ
labial	π	β	φ ⇒ ψ	φθ
velar	κ	γ	χ ⇒ ξ	χθ
dental	τ	δ	θ ⇒ σ	σθ
when aspirates are reduplicated they become unvoiced				

If two letters collide in such a way that they sound like a third letter, Greek simply replaces the two colliding letters with the letter whose sound they make.

There are two primary letters which create this collision: sigma and theta.

Addition of Sigma

Labials are made with the lips as in π, β, and φ.

Try pronouncing any labial plus sigma:

$$πσ, βσ φσ$$

Can you see why the result is a

$$ψ?$$

Velars are made in the back of the throat as in κ, γ, and χ.

Try pronouncing any velar plus sigma:

$$κσ, γσ χσ$$

Can you see why the result is a

$$ξ?$$

Dentals are made when the tongue touches the front teeth as in τ, δ, and θ.

Try pronouncing any dental plus sigma:

$$τσ, δσ θσ$$

Can you see why the result is a

$$σ?$$

The dental is dropped because it is so awkward to pronounce it before the sigma.

Addition of Theta

Square of Stops					
	unvoiced	voiced	aspirate	+ σ	+ θ
labial	π	β	φ ⇨	ψ	φθ
velar	κ	γ	χ ⇨	ξ	χθ
dental	τ	δ	θ ⇨	σ	σθ
when aspirates are reduplicated they become unvoiced					

Unvoiced consonants do not engage the vocal chords. Try pronouncing π, κ, and τ and notice that the vocal chords are not used.

Voiced consonants engage the vocal chords. Try pronouncing β, γ, and δ and notice that the vocal chords are used.

Aspirate consonants involve the flow of air. Try pronouncing φ, χ, and θ and notice the flow of air.

Interesting, eh?

Here is the general rule: When you add θ to a voiced or unvoiced aspirate, it becomes the related aspirate. For example:

When a θ is added to the labials π and β, it becomes φθ. In other words

$$\pi\theta \;\to\; \phi\theta$$
$$\beta\theta \;\to\; \phi\theta$$

When a θ is added to the velars κ and γ, it becomes χθ. In other words

$$\kappa\theta \;\to\; \chi\theta$$
$$\gamma\theta \;\to\; \chi\theta$$

When a θ is added to the dentals τ and δ, it becomes σθ. In other words

$$\tau\theta \;\rightarrow\; \sigma\theta$$
$$\delta\theta \;\rightarrow\; \sigma\theta$$

If this is overwhelming right now, don't worry. We will have the opportunity to see this again and again. You will get the hang of it.

Back to Third Declension

Noun Endings				
		Masc / Fem (3rd declension)		**Neuter** (3rd declension)
Singular	**Nominative** subject	ς	σαρξ flesh	—	φως light
	Genitive possession	ος	σαρκος of flesh	ος	φωτος of light
	Dative in, with, to, by	ι	σαρκι to flesh	ι	φωτι to light
	Accusative object	α	σαρκα flesh	—	φως light
Plural	**Nominative** subject	ες	σαρκες fleshes	α	φωτα lights
	Genitive possession	ων	σαρκων of fleshes	ων	φωτων of lights
	Dative in, with, to, by	σιν	σαρξιν to fleshes	σιν	φωσιν to lights
	Accusative object	ας	σαρκας fleshes	α	φωτα lights

The neuter noun, φῶς, is built on the stem φωτ.

It is obvious how the endings are being attached except in the nominative singular and dative plural. Remember the Square of Stops?

When sigma is added to a dental, the dental is dropped (see p. 61 above).

$$\tau\sigma \;>\; \sigma$$

So φωτς becomes φως (nominative singular)

and

φωτσιν becomes φωσιν (dative plural)

Square of Stops				
	unvoiced	voiced	aspirate	+ σ	+ θ
labial	π	β	φ	⇨ ψ	φθ
velar	κ	γ	χ	⇨ ξ	χθ
dental	τ	δ	θ	⇨ σ	σθ
when aspirates are reduplicated they become unvoiced					

Also, please notice that the <u>nominative singular forms are often odd</u> but the

genitive forms are always regular.

If you want to find out in what consonant a third declension noun ends, look at the genitive singular form. Remove the noun ending (ος) and you will see the final consonant.

Some Greek students are terrified of third declension nouns. This is a problem because there are lots of them! There is no need to fear. Although they are not as consistent as first and second declension nouns, the patterns are fairly easy to see in context.

Here are examples of masculine, feminine, and neuter third declension nouns which play by the rules: ἀνήρ, γυνή, and ὄνομα.

		Masc (3rd declension)		**F**eminine (3rd declension)		**N**euter (3rd declension)	
Singular	**Nominative** subject	ς	ἀνήρ man		γυνή woman	–	ὄνομα name
	Genitive possession	ος	ἀνδρός of man		γυναικός of woman	ος	ὀνόματος of a name
	Dative in, with, to, by	ι	ἀνδρί to man		γυναικί to woman	ι	ὀνόματι to a name
	Accusative object	α	ἄνδρα man		γυναῖκα woman	–	ὄνομα name
Plural	**Nominative** subject	ες	ἄνδρες men		γυναῖκες women	α	ὀνόματα names
	Genitive possession	ων	ανδρῶν of men		γυναικῶν of women	ων	ὀνομάτων of names
	Dative in, with, to, by	σιν	ανδράσιν to men		γυναιξίν to women	σιν	ὀνομάσιν to names
	Accusative object	ας	ἄνδρας men		γυναῖκας women	α	ὀνόματα names

Third Declension Nouns

Here are examples of some third declension nouns that do not perfectly follow the chart. However, notice the similarities.

		χάρις, ος, ἡ	πατήρ, πατρος, ὁ	ἱερεύς, έως, ὁ	γένος, ους, τό
Singular	**Nominative** subject	χάρις	πατήρ	ἱερεύς	γένος
	Genitive possession	χάριτος	πατρός	ἱερέως	γένους
	Dative in, with, to, by	χάριτι	πατρί	ἱερεῖ	γένει
	Accusative object	χάριν	πατέρα	ἱερέα	γένος
Plural	**Nominative** subject	χάριτες	πατέρες	ἱερεῖς	γένη
	Genitive possession	χαρίτων	πατέρων	ἱερέων	γενῶν
	Dative in, with, to, by	χάρισι[ν]	πατράσι[ν]	ἱερευσι[ν]	γένεσι[ν]
	Accusative object	χάριτας	πατέρας	ἱερεῖς	γένη

The best way to master third declension nouns is to read lots of Greek. And that is fun!

Let's practice our third declension with a sentence.

πίστις σῴζει ἄνδρας καὶ γυναῖκας τῇ δύναμει
faith   saves   men   and   women   by the   power

τῆς¹ χάριτος.
of   grace

word	ending	case	function in sentence
πίστις	ς	nominative	subject
ἄνδρας καὶ γυναῖκας	ας	accusative (plural)	object
χάριτος	ος	genitive	possession
δύναμει	ι	dative	indirect object

Noun Endings				
		Masc/**F**em (3rd declension)		**N**euter (3rd declension)
Singular	**Nominative** subject	ς	σαρξ flesh	— light / φως light
	Genitive possession	ος	σαρκος of flesh	ος	φωτος of light
	Dative in, with, to, by	ι	σαρκι to flesh	ι	φωτι to light
	Accusative object	α	σαρκα flesh	—	φως light
Plural	**Nominative** subject	ες	σαρκες fleshes	α	φωτα lights
	Genitive possession	ων	σαρκων of fleshes	ων	φωτων of lights
	Dative in, with, to, by	σιν	σαρξιν to fleshes	σιν	φωσιν to lights
	Accusative object	ας	σαρκας fleshes	α	φωτα lights

In this example, the Greek word order is similar to English so the translation is easy:

Faith saves men and women by the power of grace.

---

¹ Notice that we do not translate the article. Abstract nouns in Greek often have the article in Greek. We do not use in in English.

Conclusion

So there you have it: The syntax and morphology of Greek nouns.

You may be blown away by this week. Do not be discouraged! As we continue on together we will see this over and over. You will learn to recognize these patterns and it will start to make sense.

If you have never studied a highly inflected language (where words change forms a lot) these ideas are completely new to you. No not worry if you find it difficult. That is normal!

We are developing uncharted areas of your mind. This is a good thing! Your brain is getting bigger. Pretty soon you will look like those really smart aliens on Star Trek.

Camp Modifier

The Article and Adjectives

11. The Article

Lesson in a Nutshell

> The article (and all modifiers) match the nouns they modify in case, number and gender. They must be able to be masculine **and** feminine **and** neuter nouns. The article changes form ("declines") according to a 2-1-2 pattern.

English Articles: "A" and "The"

In English there are two kinds of articles, the definite article ("the") and the indefinite article ("a").

The definite article "definitizes." It points to something specifically. Not just any old tree,"*the*" tree. Not just any old monkey, "*the*" monkey.

The indefinite article leaves options open. "A" tree, meaning any old tree. "A" monkey, meaning any old monkey.

If I ask you to bring me a cup of coffee you grab any cup and bring it to me, filled with coffee.

But if I ask you to bring me the cup of coffee, I have a specific cup of coffee in mind. The definite article takes the general concept and "definitizes" it.

If you are an English speaker you will find this all very natural.

The Greek Article: Three Twists

As we go along, we will find that the Greek article is very helpful in our translation. But there are three twists to the Greek article we must get used to.

Twist #1: No Indefinite Article

There is no indefinite article in Greek. In other words, there is no form of the article specifically to designate that you mean "a" monkey. Or, if you prefer, there is no way to be specifically non-specific.

So how does Greek communicate an indefinite idea? Usually by not using the article at all.

ὁ ανθρωπος = "the" man.

ανθρωπος = "a" man

This is not a hard and fast rule. We will discover many exceptions as we go along.

For example, John 1:1 reads as follows:

$$\text{\_\_ θεὸς ἦν ὁ λόγος}$$
God   was the Word

There is no article before θεος ("God"). Does this mean that "God" is indefinite here, in other words, that the Word was a god? If so, then Jesus may be god-like but John is not claiming that he is fully God. This would be contrary to other things that John says about Jesus in his gospel.

What is going on here?

This is an example of the nuanced way that Greek makes use of the article.

One cannot automatically assume that if there is no article that the noun is indefinite ("a").

One cannot automatically assume that if there is an article that we supply the definite article in our translation ("the").

John has crafted a remarkably nuanced statement about the nature of Jesus in four words. We will study this more in our next class, *Studies in John*.

Twist #2: Greater Nuance

Greek use of the article is much more nuanced than in English. There are similarities with the use of the English article. But there are also many ways in which the Greek article is used differently than the English article. The only way to get the hang of it will be to read a lot of Greek.

Twist #3: 24 Forms

There are 24 forms of the Greek article.[1] In other words, there are 24 ways to say "the."

Huh??　　　　　　　Why??

Because in English we use the word "the" whether we are talking about...

the man
the men

the woman
the women

the work
the works

The English article does not change form to match the case, number and gender of the noun it modifies. But in Greek, the article looks like this:

ὁ ανθρωπος	the man
οἱ ανθρωποι	the men
ἡ γυνη	the woman
αἱ γυναι	the women
τό εργον	the work
τά εργα	the works

See how the Greek article changes form? The boring old English article remains static. The fascinating Greek article changes form to match the noun it modifies in case, number and gender.

---

[1] There are actually fewer forms since some of them repeat, but I find it helpful to think of it this way.

I'll say it again: The article is changing forms to match the noun it modifies in:

case (nominative, genitive, dative, accusative)
number (singular, plural)
gender (masculine, feminine, neuter)

Let's take a look at how the article "morphs" to do this.

Article Morphology

We saw that every noun has case, number and gender. The same will be true with the article.

But there were only eight forms of each noun. There are 24 forms of the article. Why?

Because the nouns were either masculine or feminine or neuter.

But the article has to be able to modify all kinds of nouns. This is why it must be able to be masculine and feminine and neuter.

So rather than eight forms there are 3 x 8 forms = 24.

$$2 \text{ (numbers)} \quad \text{X} \quad 3 \text{ (genders)} \quad \text{X} \quad 4 \text{ (cases)} \quad = \quad 24 \text{ (forms)}$$

That's…

2 (numbers)

Two Numbers

The Article			M	F	N
Singular	Nominative	"the"	ὁ	ἡ	τό
	Genitive	"of the"	τοῦ	τῆς	τοῦ
	Dative	"to the"	τῷ	τῇ	τῷ
	Accusative	the	τόν	τήν	τό
Plural	Nominative	"the"	οἱ	αἱ	τά
	Genitive	"of the"	τῶν	τῶν	τῶν
	Dative	"to the"	τοῖς	ταῖς	τοῖς
	Accusative	"the"	τούς	τάς	τά

x 3 (genders)

Three Genders

The Article			M	F	N
Singular	Nominative	"the"	ὁ	ἡ	τό
	Genitive	"of the"	τοῦ	τῆς	τοῦ
	Dative	"to the"	τῷ	τῇ	τῷ
	Accusative	the	τόν	τήν	τό
Plural	Nominative	"the"	οἱ	αἱ	τά
	Genitive	"of the"	τῶν	τῶν	τῶν
	Dative	"to the"	τοῖς	ταῖς	τοῖς
	Accusative	"the"	τούς	τάς	τά

x 4 (cases)

Four Cases

The Article			M	F	N
Singular	Nominative	"the"	ὁ	ἡ	τό
	Genitive	"of the"	τοῦ	τῆς	τοῦ
	Dative	"to the"	τῷ	τῇ	τῷ
	Accusative	the	τόν	τήν	τό
Plural	Nominative	"the"	οἱ	αἱ	τά
	Genitive	"of the"	τῶν	τῶν	τῶν
	Dative	"to the"	τοῖς	ταῖς	τοῖς
	Accusative	"the"	τούς	τάς	τά

$$= 24 \text{ (forms)}$$

This is what the 24 forms look like

The Article			M	F	N
Singular	Nominative "the"		ὁ	ἡ	τό
	Genitive "of the"		τοῦ	τῆς	τοῦ
	Dative "to the"		τῷ	τῇ	τῷ
	Accusative the		τόν	τήν	τό
Plural	Nominative "the"		οἱ	αἱ	τά
	Genitive "of the"		τῶν	τῶν	τῶν
	Dative "to the"		τοῖς	ταῖς	τοῖς
	Accusative "the"		τούς	τάς	τά

At this point you may be terrified. If there are so many forms of Greek words, what hope is there of ever learning all this!

Don't panic.

It is not nearly as bad as it sounds. The patterns that Greek words follow to tell you their case, number and gender are very regular. In fact, we already know them!

Compare the forms of the article with the noun endings table:

The Article			M (2)	F (1)	N (2)
Singular	Nominative "the"		ὁ	ἡ	τό
	Genitive "of the"		τοῦ	τῆς	τοῦ
	Dative "to the"		τῷ	τῇ	τῷ
	Accusative the		τόν	τήν	τό
Plural	Nominative "the"		οἱ	αἱ	τά
	Genitive "of the"		τῶν	τῶν	τῶν
	Dative "to the"		τοῖς	ταῖς	τοῖς
	Accusative "the"		τούς	τάς	τά

Noun Endings					
Masculine (2nd declension)		Feminine (1st declension)		Neuter (2nd declension)	
ος	λογος word	α or η	αρχη beginning	ον	εργον work
ου	λογου of a word	ας or ης	αρχης of a beginning	ου	εργου of work
ῳ	λογῳ to a word	ᾳ or ῃ	αρχῃ to a beginning	ῳ	εργῳ to work
ον	λογον word	αν or ην	αρχην beginning	ον	εργον work
οι	λογοι words	αι	αρχαι beginnings	α	εργα works
ων	λογων of words	ων	αρχων of beginnings	ων	εργων of works
οις	λογοις to words	αις	αρχαις to beginnings	οις	εργοις to works
ους	λογους words	ας	αρχας beginnings	α	εργα works

Do you see the similarities? In most instances, the article looks like the noun ending with a tau attached to the front. Again, mastering Greek is all about learning to see patterns!

Lexical Form of The Article

When you look up the Greek article in a lexicon, it is listed like this:

ὁ, ἡ, τό

Why three forms? Because to know the article we have to know how it behaves in its masculine, feminine and neuter forms. The lexicon gives us this information.

The article follows a 2-1-2 pattern. This means it follows the second declension in the masculine gender, the first declension in the feminine gender and the second declension in the neuter gender.

	Masculine	Feminine	Neuter
2-1-2	2nd declension	1st declension	2nd declension

More about this in our next lesson.

12. 2-1-2 Adjectives

Lesson in a Nutshell

2-1-2 adjectives follow the 2-1-2 pattern of declension. They are by far the most common.

When you look up the adjective ἀγαθός in the lexicon, it will be listed like this:

$$\text{ἀγαθός, ή, όν}$$

Please notice that there is no article. Why?

Because ἀγαθός is not a noun. It is not masculine <u>or</u> feminine <u>or</u> neuter.

ἄγαθος is an adjective. It has to be able to be masculine <u>AND</u> feminine <u>AND</u> neuter.

The lexicon gives you the endings (in red above) to tell you how it behaves in all three genders.

ἀγαθός is the masculine form

ἀγαθή is the feminine form

ἀγαθόν is the neuter form

ἀγαθός is a 2-1-2 adjective. This means it follows

second declension in the masculine (2)

first declension in the feminine, and (1)

second declension in the neuter (2)

Just like the article!

Do you see why we must have all three genders? Because "good" needs to be able to modify masculine <u>and</u> feminine <u>and</u> neuter nouns. This is unlike English. English has only one form. Compare the English adjective "good" with the Greek adjective ἀγαθος.

Case, Number, Gender	Greek	English
nominative, singular, masculine	ἀγαθος ἄνθρωπος	<u>good</u> man
nominative, plural, masculine	ἀγαθοι ἄνθρωποι	<u>good</u> men
nominative, singular, feminine	ἀγαθη γύνη	<u>good</u> woman
nominative, plural, feminine	ἀγαθαι γύναι	<u>good</u> women
nominative or accusative, singular, neuter	ἀγαθον ἔργον	<u>good</u> work
nominative or accusative, plural, neuter	ἀγαθα ἔργα	<u>good</u> works
genitive, singular, neuter	ἀγαθου ἔργου	of a <u>good</u> work
dative, singular, neuter	ἀγαθῷ ἐργῷ	to a <u>good</u> work

Do you see how "good" never changes form, but ἀγαθος is constantly changing to match the noun it modifies?

Now the lights are going on!

Notice how the endings follow the 2-1-2 pattern (in blue). Also, compare the endings of ἀγαθός with the article below. Do you see how similar the endings are?

24 forms of ἀγαθός [2-1-2]

	Masculine	Feminine	Neuter
n	αγαθος	αγαθη	αγαθον
g	αγαθου	αγαθης	αγαθου
d	αγαθω	αγαθη	αγαθω
a	αγαθον	αγαθην	αγαθον
n	αγαθοι	αγαθαι	αγαθα
g	αγαθων	αγαθων	αγαθων
d	αγαθοις	αγαθαις	αγαθοις
a	αγαθους	αγαθας	αγαθα

Case Endings

		Masculine 2	Feminine 1	Neuter 2	Masc/Fem 3	Neuter 3
Singular	Nominative subject	ος	α or η	ον	ς	–
	Genitive possession	ου	ας or ης	ου	ος	ος
	Dative in, with, to, by	ῳ	ᾳ or η	ῳ	ι	ι
	Accusative object	ον	αν or ην	ον	α	–
Plural	Nominative subject	οι	αι	α	ες	α
	Genitive possession	ων	ων	ων	ων	ων
	Dative in, with, to, by	οις	αις	οις	σιν	σιν
	Accusative object	ους	ας	α	ας	α

The Article

			M	F	N
Singular	Nominative	"the"	ὁ	ἡ	τό
	Genitive	"of the"	τοῦ	τῆς	τοῦ
	Dative	"to the"	τῷ	τῇ	τῷ
	Accusative	the	τόν	τήν	τό
Plural	Nominative	"the"	οἱ	αἱ	τά
	Genitive	"of the"	τῶν	τῶν	τῶν
	Dative	"to the"	τοῖς	ταῖς	τοῖς
	Accusative	"the"	τούς	τάς	τά

Greek may seem complicated at first. But as you go along, you will come to recognize a few consistent patterns that reveal the case, number and gender of every substantive. It will become as plain as the nose on your face.

Please study the chart below and be certain that all the letters in green make sense to you. Be sure you understand:

1. That they follow the 2-1-2 pattern of declension.

2. That the articles and adjectives match the noun they modify in case, number and gender.

3. The translations.

		the good word / beginning / work					
		Masculine (2nd declension)		**F**eminine (1st declension)		**N**euter (2nd declension)	
Singular	N	ος	ὁ ἀγαθός λόγος the good word	α..η	ἡ ἀγαθή ἀρχή the good beginning	ον	τό ἀγαθόν ἔργον the good work
	G	ου	τοῦ ἀγαθοῦ λόγου of the good word	ας.ης	τῆς ἀγαθῆς ἀρχῆς of the good beginning	ου	τοῦ ἀγαθοῦ ἔργου of the good work
	D	ῳ	τῷ ἀγαθῷ λόγῳ to the good word	α..η	τῇ ἀγαθῇ ἀρχῇ to the good beginning	ῳ	τῷ ἀγαθῷ ἔργῳ to the good work
	A	ον	τόν ἀγαθόν λόγον the good word	αν. or ην	τήν ἀγαθήν ἀρχήν the good beginning	ον	τό ἀγαθόν ἔργον the good work
Plural	N	οι	οἱ ἀγαθοί λόγοι the good words	αι	αἱ ἀγαθαί ἀρχαί the good beginnings	α	τά ἀγαθά ἔργα the good works
	G	ων	τῶν ἀγαθῶν λόγων of the good words	ων	τῶν ἀγαθῶν ἀρχῶν of the good beginnings	ων	τῶν ἀγαθῶν ἔργων of the good works
	D	οις	τοῖς ἀγαθοῖς λόγοις to the good words	αις	ταῖς ἀγαθαῖς ἀρχαῖς to the good beginnings	οις	τοῖς ἀγαθοῖς ἔργοις to the good works
	A	ους	τούς ἀγαθούς λόγους the good words	ας	τάς ἀγαθάς ἀρχάς the good beginnings	α	τά ἀγαθά ἔργα the good works

13. 3-1-3 Adjectives

Lesson in a Nutshell

3-1-3 adjectives follow a 3-1-3 pattern of declension. Πας is an important 3-1-3 adjective.

If the table below makes sense to you, you already understand 3-1-3 adjectives. The rest is just filling in a few details.

	Masculine	Feminine	Neuter
2-1-2 adjectives	**2nd** declension	**1st** declension	**2nd** declension
3-1-3 adjectives	**3rd** declension	**1st** declension	**3rd** declension

We saw that 2-1-2 adjectives followed the
    second declension in the masculine
    first declension in the feminine, and
    second declension in the neuter

3-1-3 adjectives follow the
    third declension in the masculine
    first declension in the feminine, and
    third declension in the neuter

πᾶς means "all" or "every" and is a common 3-1-3 adjective. Do you see how the case endings were tacked onto πᾶς in the tables below? (Look at the blue columns.)

24 forms of πας (3-1-3)			
	3 masc	**1 fem**	**3 neut**
N	πας	πασα	παν
G	παντος	πασης	παντος
D	παντι	παση	παντι
A	παντα	πασαν	παν
N	παντες	πασαι	παντα
G	παντων	πασων	παντων
D	πασι[ν]	πασαις	πασι[ν]
A	παντας	πασας	παντα

Case Endings							
		Masculine **2**	**F**eminine **1**	**N**euter **2**		**M**asc/ **F**em **3**	**N**euter **3**
Singular	Nominative subject	ος	α.η	ον		ς	—
	Genitive possession	ου	ας.ης	ου		ος	ος
	Dative in, with, to, by	ω	α.η	ω		ι	ι
	Accusative object	ον	αν.ην	ον		α	—
Plural	Nominative subject	οι	αι	α		ες	α
	Genitive possession	ων	ων	ων		ων	ων
	Dative in, with, to, by	οις	αις	οις		σιν	σιν
	Accusative object	ους	ας	α		ας	α

In case you were wondering...

We saw that third declension <u>nouns</u> were those whose stem ended in a consonant. 3-1-3 <u>adjectives</u> follow the third declension in the masculine and neuter genders for the same reason: those two stems end in a consonant. Observe:

stem in masculine gender	stem in feminine gender	stem in neuter gender
παντ	πασα	παντ

Do you see how the masculine and neuter forms end in a consonant (τ)? This is the reason they follow third declension in those genders.

The feminine form ends in a vowel (α) so it follows first declension, which is used for stems that end in the vowels α or η.

How perfectly logical!

When we were looking at third declension nouns, we saw that the third declension is not as consistent as first and second declension.

The same thing is true with adjectives that follow the third declension. τάχυς means "fast" or "quick" and is a 3-1-3 adjective. Notice the slightly strange forms (in red).

ταχύς (3-1-3)

	3 masc	1 fem	3 neut
N	ταχυς	ταχεια	ταχυ
G	ταχεως	ταχειας	ταχεως
D	ταχει	ταχεια	ταχει
A	ταχυν	ταχειαν	ταχυ
N	ταχεις	ταχειαι	ταχεα
G	ταχεων	ταχειων	ταχεων
D	ταχεσι [v]	ταχειαις	ταχεσι [v]
A	ταχεις	ταχειας	ταχεα

Case Endings

		Masculine 2	Feminine 1	Neuter 2	Masc/Fem 3	Neuter 3
Singular	Nominative subject	ος	α, η	ον	ς	—
	Genitive possession	ου	ας, ης	ου	ος	ος
	Dative in, with, to, by	ῳ	ᾳ, η	ῳ	ι	ι
	Accusative object	ον	αν, ην	ον	α	—
Plural	Nominative subject	οι	αι	α	ες	α
	Genitive possession	ων	ων	ων	ων	ων
	Dative in, with, to, by	οις	αις	οις	σιν	σιν
	Accusative object	ους	ας	α	ας	α

We have already seen this sort of odd behavior when we looked at third declension nouns.

Thankfully, most adjectives follow the 2-1-2 pattern.

Lexical Form

When you look up the adjective πᾶς in the lexicon, it will be listed like this.

πᾶς, πᾶσα, πᾶν

Notice that there is no article. Why?

Because πᾶς is not a noun. It is not masculine <u>or</u> feminine <u>or</u> neuter.

πᾶς is an adjective. It has to be able to be masculine <u>AND</u> feminine <u>AND</u> neuter.

The lexicon lists the three genders to show you how it behaves in all three genders.

πᾶς is a 3-1-3 adjective. This means it follows

third declension in the masculine (3)
first declension in the feminine, and (1)
third declension in the neuter (3)

Note: *There are relatively few 3-1-3 adjectives. So why bother with them? Because when we come to the participle, this pattern will be very important to recognize. But don't worry about participles yet! All in good time.*

14. 2-2 & 3-3 Adjectives

Lesson in a Nutshell

2-2 adjectives follow second declension in all three genders. This is normal for the masculine and neuter, but looks odd in the feminine.

3-3 adjectives are third declension in all three genders.

A reminder: All we are doing is studying the patterns by which adjectives tell us their case, number, and gender.

We have seen the behavior of 2-1-2 and 3-1-3 adjectives.

2-2 and 3-3 adjectives may strike you as strange. There are three genders. Why only two numbers to designate three genders?

Because in the case of 2-2 and 3-3- adjectives, the first number tells us how the adjective behaves in masculine **and feminine** genders. The second number tells us how the adjective behaves in the neuter gender.

	Masculine	Feminine	Neuter
2-1-2 adjectives	**2nd** declension	**1st** declension	**2nd** declension
3-1-3 adjectives	**3rd** declension	**1st** declension	**3rd** declension
2-2 adjectives	**2nd** declension		**2nd** declension
3-3 adjectives	**3rd** declension		**3rd** declension

Let's take a closer look.

2-2 Pattern

ἁμαρτωλός, -όν

ἁμαρτωλός is a 2-2 adjective that means "sinful." It is called a 2-2 adjective because it follows...

second declension in the masculine <u>and feminine</u> gender and
second declension in the neuter.

The pattern is a little strange to us because the feminine is usually first declension, not second.

ἁμαρτωλός [2-2]

	(2) Masculine <u>and</u> (2) Feminine	(2) Neuter
n	ἁμαρτωλ**ος**	ἁμαρτωλ**ον**
g	ἁμαρτωλ**ου**	ἁμαρτωλ**ου**
d	ἁμαρτωλ**ῳ**	ἁμαρτωλ**ῳ**
a	ἁμαρτωλ**ον**	ἁμαρτωλ**ον**
n	ἁμαρτωλ**οι**	ἁμαρτωλ**α**
g	ἁμαρτωλ**ων**	ἁμαρτωλ**ων**
d	ἁμαρτωλ**οις**	ἁμαρτωλ**οις**
a	ἁμαρτωλ**ους**	ἁμαρτωλ**α**

Case Endings

		Masculine Feminine 2	Feminine 1	Neuter 2	Masc/Fem 3	Neuter 3
Singular	**Nominative** subject	ος	α or η	ον	ς	–
	Genitive possession	ου	ας or ης	ου	ος	ος
	Dative in, with, to, by	ῳ	ᾳ or η	ῳ	ι	ι
	Accusative object	ον	αν or ην	ον	α	–
Plural	**Nominative** subject	οι	αι	α	ες	α
	Genitive possession	ων	ων	ων	ων	ων
	Dative in, with, to, by	οις	αις	οις	σιν	σιν
	Accusative object	ους	ας	α	ας	α

Study these two tables until it makes sense to you how the endings in blue are added to the adjective.

3-3 Pattern

μείζων, -ον

μείζων means "greater" and is a 3-3 adjective. This means it follows

third declension in the masculine <u>and feminine</u> gender, and
third declension in the neuter.

Do you see how the case endings (in blue) are attached to the adjective?

μείζων [3-3]

	(3) Masculine <u>and</u> (3) Feminine	(3) Neuter
n	μειζ**ων**	μειζ**ον**
g	μειζο**νος**	μειζο**νος**
d	μειζο**νι**	μειζο**νι**
a	μειζο**να**	μειζ**ον**
n	μειζο**νες**	μειζο**να**
g	μειζο**νων**	μειζο**νων**
d	μειζο**σι**[v]	μειζο**σι**[v]
a	μειζο**νας**	μειζο**να**

Case Endings

		Masculine 2	Feminine 1	Neuter 2	Masc/Fem 3	Neuter 3
Singular	Nominative subject	ος	α or η	ον	ς	--
	Genitive possession	ου	ας or ης	ου	ος	ος
	Dative in, with, to, by	ῳ	ᾳ or η	ῳ	ι	ι
	Accusative object	ον	αν or ην	ον	α	--
Plural	Nominative subject	οι	αι	α	ες	α
	Genitive possession	ων	ων	ων	ων	ων
	Dative in, with, to, by	οις	αις	οις	σιν	σιν
	Accusative object	ους	ας	α	ας	α

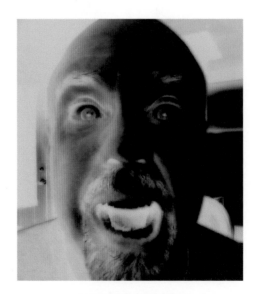

Don't be afraid!

Lexical Form of Adjectives

How will you know what pattern an adjective follows? The lexicon will tell you by the way it lists the adjective and if this leaves things unclear, it will list a few more examples to help.

Here are the adjectives we have studied as they are listed in the lexicon.

2-1-2	3-1-3	2-2	3-3
ἀληθινός , -ή, -όν	πᾶς, πᾶσα, πᾶν	ἁμαρτωλός, -όν	μείζων, -ον

The lexicon will list the adjective in its masculine, feminine, and neuter forms.

If the masculine and feminine share a form, the first entry will refer to the masculine **and feminine** forms. The second entry will refer to the neuter form.

How will you tell an adjective from a noun? A <u>noun will always be listed with an article</u>. A noun is **either** masculine **or** feminine **or** neuter. The article tells you the gender of the noun.

An adjective has to be able to change forms to match all three genders. It is necessary to understand the pattern it follows in the masculine **and** feminine **and** neuter genders.

Odd Patterns

Almost every time, you will be able to identify the case, number and gender of an adjective using the case endings chart. But not all adjectives follow the case endings exactly.

Don't worry. It is usually very easy to figure out the case, number and gender of adjectives.

15. Adjective Usage

Lesson in a Nutshell

Adjectives may be attributive, substantival, or predicate.

Usage	Definition	English Example
1. Attributive Adjectives	"attribute" some quality to a noun	the good man
2. Substantival Adjectives	"stand in" for a noun.	God rewards the good.
3. Predicate Adjectives	involve some form of "to be"	God is good.

The article is an important clue to determine what kind of adjective it is.

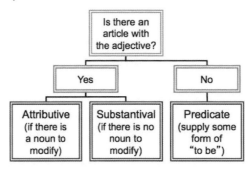

Adjectives are words that modify nouns. They give us useful clarification about the noun in question. Greek adjectives are very similar to English adjectives with the exception we have come to expect: Greek adjectives change forms to show us their case, number and gender.

This lesson focuses on the three ways that adjectives are used in Greek

Usage	Definition	English Example
1. Attributive Adjectives	"attribute" some quality to a noun"	the good man
2. Substantival Adjectives	"stand in" for a noun.	God rewards the good.
3. Predicate Adjectives	involve some form of "to be"	God is good.

Attributive Adjectives

Attributive adjectives modify a noun. They "attribute" some quality to a noun.

The green tree
The little grammar
The lovely wife

In English, the adjective immediately precedes the noun it modifies (word order again!)
In Greek, attributive adjectives may follow English word order or may reveal themselves
in other ways.

Here is an example that follows English word order:

ὁ ἀγαθός ἄνθρωπος
the   good   man

Here is another common example of an attributive adjective that is unlike English word
order:

ὁ ἄνθρωπος ὁ ἀγαθός
the   man   (the)   good

Attributive adjectives usually have the article.

Substantival Adjectives

Substantival adjectives "stand in" for nouns. They have substance!

The diligent will do well in this class.

Diligent what? Students, of course. But the word "student" is not in this sentence. It is
assumed. The adjective is left on its own, and performs the function of the noun in the
sentence.

Here are a few more examples of substantival adjectives.

The righteous are treated better than the sinful.
The good, the bad, and the ugly.

If there is no noun to modify, the adjective takes on substance of its own — a
substantival adjective!

Here are a few examples in Greek.

ὁ ἀγαθός ζήσει
the good (man) will live

ἡ ἀγαθή ζήσει
the good (woman) will live

αἱ ἀγαθάι ζήσει
the good (women) will live

The case, number and gender will match the missing noun. Notice in the examples above that

In the first example ἀγαθός is singular masculine so we assume a singular masculine subject.

In the second example ἀγαθή is singular feminine so we assume a singular feminine subject.

In the third example ἀγαθάι is feminine plural so we assume a feminine plural subject.

Substantival adjectives usually have the article.

If there is no noun for an adjective to modify there is a good chance it is substantival.

Predicate Adjectives

Predicate adjectives involve some form of "to be." For example,

The man is good.
That ice cream was delicious!

In Greek, it looks like this:

ὁ ἀνθρωπός ἐστίν ἀγαθός
the   man   is   good

ὁ ἀνθρωπός ἀγαθός
the   man   (is) good

In the first example, the "to-be" verb is expressed (ἐστίν "is"). In the second, it is not. Greek will often leave the verb unexpressed if it believes it to be obvious.

The predicate adjective
<u>never</u>
has the article.

To summarize…

Usage	Definition	English Example
Attributive Adjectives	"attribute" some quality to a noun"	the good man
Substantival Adjectives	"stand in" for a noun	God rewards the good.
Predicate Adjectives	involve some form of "to be"	God is good.

The article is an important clue to determine what kind of adjective it is.

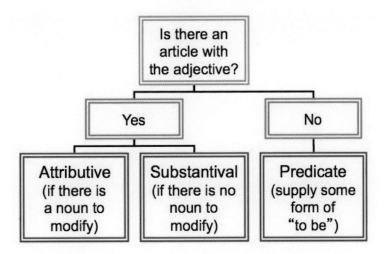

Pronoun Point

Pronouns!

16. First & Second Person Pronouns

Lesson in a Nutshell

In Greek, first and second person pronouns do not have gender so there are only eight forms.

1st Person				2nd Person			
Singular	Nom	ἐγώ	I	**Singular**	Nom	σύ	you
	Gen	μου ἐμοῦ	my		Gen	σου σοῦ	your
	Dat	μοι ἐμοί	to me		Dat	σοι σοί	to you
	Acc	με ἐμέ	me		Acc	σε σέ	you
Plural	Nom	ἡμεῖς	we	**Plural**	Nom	ὑμεῖς	you
	Gen	ἡμῶν	our		Gen	ὑμῶν	your
	Dat	ἡμῖν	to us		Dat	ὑμῖν	to you
	Acc	ἡμᾶς	us		Acc	ὑμᾶς	you

Pronouns are everywhere! There are not very many of them, but you will see them splattered on every page. Even in English they are extremely common. I have highlighted them in these first few paragraphs so you can see that it is true.

It is critical to recognize pronouns in their various forms. They are so important that on your Master Chart I have spelled out eleven of the most common pronouns in every possible form and translated them for you.

We have seen all of these variations before. Most pronouns follow the nice, simple 2-1-2 pattern of declension.

Please keep in mind that the pronouns on the Master Chart represent **only eleven words**. Do not fear! Each box represents a single word in all of its forms. We have already met the forms. There is no need to fear.

Syntax

Pronouns are the little words that "stand in" for nouns in all kinds of interesting ways. There are different varieties of pronouns: personal, relative, interrogative, indefinite, demonstrative and reflexive. Each has its own function, as we will see.

Morphology

Pronouns must be able to "stand in" for all kinds of subjects: masculine, feminine and neuter. Therefore, they will be like adjectives. There will be up to 24 forms of each pronoun, depending on which pattern of declension it follows.

The Concept of "Person"

Before examining the personal pronouns, we must pause to understand what is meant by "person." Here is a chart of personal pronouns in English.

	Singular	**Plural**
First Person I We	N: I G: mine D: to me A: me	N: we G: our D: to us A: us
Second Person You You	N: you G: your D: to you A: you	N: you G: your D: to you A: you
Third Person He-She-It They	N: he-she-it G: his-hers-its D: to him-her-it A: him-her-it	N: they G: theirs D: to them A: them

Notice three odd things about English personal pronouns.

1. Unlike most English words, they decline a lot and in ways that follow no clear pattern. It's positively barbaric!

2. The second person pronoun is the same in the singular and plural (unless you are from the South, in which case you say "y'all" for the second person plural).

3. In the third person singular <u>only</u>, English pronouns have gender. This is why there are three forms ("he-she-it").

Greek pronouns are much more civilized. Here are the Greek first and second person pronouns.

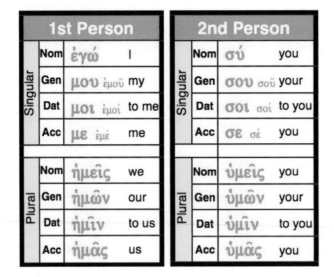

Please notice that there are only

      eight forms of the first person pronoun, and

      eight forms of the second person pronoun.

           Do you see why? What is missing?

      There are only eight forms because in Greek, first and second pronouns

do not have gender!

The first and second person personal pronouns follow a slightly odd third declension pattern. It is best just to memorize them. You will see them on every page so do yourself a favor and make friends with them.

Notice how similar the first and second person pronouns are to each other. There is just a letter's difference between them in most cases.

The forms in small print are emphatic forms. For example, μου means "my" but ἐμοῦ means "**my!**"

In the English translations, notice that English pronouns change form ("decline") quite a bit in the first person but not in the second person.

17. Third Person Pronouns

Lesson in a Nutshell

The third person pronoun has gender and follows the familiar 2-1-2 pattern

3rd Person Pronoun						
		M (2)		F (1)		N (2)
Singular	Nom	αὐτός he	αὐτή she	αὐτό it
	Gen	αὐτοῦ his	αὐτῆς hers	αὐτοῦ its
	Dat	αὐτῷ to him	αὐτῇ to her	αὐτῷ to it
	Acc	αὐτόν him	αὐτήν her	αὐτό it
Plural	Nom	αὐτοί they	αὐταί they	αὐτά they
	Gen	αὐτῶν of them	αὐτῶν of them	αὐτῶν of them
	Dat	αὐτοῖς to them	αὐταῖς to them	αὐτοῖς to them
	Acc	αὐτούς them	αὐτάς them	αὐτά them

As a reminder, the English third person pronouns are in blue.

	Singular	Plural
First Person I We	N: I G: mine D: to me A: me	N: we G: our D: to us A: us
Second Person You You	N: you G: your D: to you A: you	N: you G: your D: to you A: you
Third Person He-She-It They	N: he-she-it G: his-hers-its D: to him-her-it A: him-her-it	N: they G: theirs D: to them A: them

As we are learning to expect, Greek third person pronouns are much more consistent. They have gender for both singular and plural forms and follow a nice easy 2-1-2 pattern of declension.

3rd Person Pronoun

		M (2)		F (1)		N (2)	
Singular	Nom	αὐτός	he	αὐτή	she	αὐτό	it
	Gen	αὐτοῦ	his	αὐτῆς	hers	αὐτοῦ	its
	Dat	αὐτῷ	to him	αὐτῇ	to her	αὐτῷ	to it
	Acc	αὐτόν	him	αὐτήν	her	αὐτό	it
Plural	Nom	αὐτοί	they	αὐταί	they	αὐτά	they
	Gen	αὐτῶν	of them	αὐτῶν	of them	αὐτῶν	of them
	Dat	αὐτοῖς	to them	αὐταῖς	to them	αὐτοῖς	to them
	Acc	αὐτούς	them	αὐτάς	them	αὐτά	them

It would be difficult to overemphasize the importance of the third person pronoun.

It shows up in nearly every line of Greek text.

The third person pronoun follows a nice easy 2-1-2 pattern of declension. In fact, it looks very much like the article with αὐ added to the front. Take some time comparing these three charts.

The Article

			M (2)	F (1)	N (2)
Singular	**Nominative**	"the"	ὁ	ἡ	τό
	Genitive	"of the"	τοῦ	τῆς	τοῦ
	Dative	"to the"	τῷ	τῇ	τῷ
	Accusative	the	τόν	τήν	τό
Plural	**Nominative**	"the"	οἱ	αἱ	τά
	Genitive	"of the"	τῶν	τῶν	τῶν
	Dative	"to the"	τοῖς	ταῖς	τοῖς
	Accusative	"the"	τούς	τάς	τά

Noun Endings

		M (2)	F (1)	N (2)
Singular	**Nominative** subject	ος	α.η	ον
	Genitive possession	ου	ας.ης	ου
	Dative in, with, to, by	ῳ	ᾳ.η	ῳ
	Accusative object	ον	αν.ην	ον
Plural	**Nominative** subject	οι	αι	α
	Genitive possession	ων	ων	ων
	Dative in, with, to, by	οις	αις	οις
	Accusative object	ους	ας	α

3rd Person Pronoun

		M (2)		F (1)		N (2)	
Singular	**Nom**	αὐτός	he	αὐτή	she	αὐτό	it
	Gen	αὐτοῦ	his	αὐτῆς	hers	αὐτοῦ	its
	Dat	αὐτῷ	to him	αὐτῇ	to her	αὐτῷ	to it
	Acc	αὐτόν	him	αὐτήν	her	αὐτό	it
Plural	**Nom**	αὐτοί	they	αὐταί	they	αὐτά	they
	Gen	αὐτῶν	of them	αὐτῶν	of them	αὐτῶν	of them
	Dat	αὐτοῖς	to them	αὐταῖς	to them	αὐτοῖς	to them
	Acc	αὐτούς	them	αὐτάς	them	αὐτά	them

The pronoun will take the case, number, and gender of the noun it "stands in" for (called its "antecedent").

The Greek third person pronoun is perfectly logical. The reason third person pronouns are difficult for English speakers is not because of Greek but because of English.

I provide you with the full paradigms and translations for all of the pronouns so you can get used to the English. The Greek is easy!

Three Uses of αὐτός

In Greek, the third person pronoun is *usually* used as a pronoun, but there are two additional functions to watch out for.

1. αὐτός as a personal pronoun (normal)

John 1 is full of examples of this. There are three in verse 12.

12 ὅσοι δὲ ἔλαβον αὐτόν, ἔδωκεν αὐτοῖς ἐξουσίαν
As many but (they) received him He gave to them authority

τέκνα θεοῦ γενέσθαι, τοῖς πιστεύουσιν εἰς τὸ ὄνομα
children of God to become, to the ones believing in the name

αὐτοῦ,
of Him,

Do you see how

the <u>accusative</u> case is used for the direct object (αὐτόν)?

the <u>dative</u> case is used for the indirect object (αὐτοῖς)?

the <u>genitive</u> case is used for possession (αὐτοῦ)?

In each instance, the pronoun is behaving just like it would in English — as a personal pronoun.

2. αὐτός **for emphasis**

Sometimes, αὐτός is used to emphasize the subject. In translation, we use some form of "self" (myself, himself, herself, itself, themselves…)

ἔγω **αὐτός** διδάσκω κοίνη ὑμίν
I **myself** am teaching Koine to you.

αὐτός ὁ πατὴρ φιλεῖ ὑμᾶς
Himself the father loves you.
= "The father himself loves you"

When used this way, αὐτός will never have the article.[1]

3. αὐτός **meaning "the same…"**

Every now and then, you will run into αὐτός and it should be translated "the same_____."

Here are a couple of examples:

καὶ πάλιν ἀπελθὼν προσηύξατο τὸν **αὐτόν** λόγον
and again leaving he prayed the **same** word

Διαιρέσεις χαρισμάτων εἰσίν, τὸ δὲ **αὐτὸ** πνεῦμα
Varieties of gifts there are the but **same** Spirit

This is the rarest uses of αὐτός. We will not run into it in John 1.

---

[1] When a substantive lacks the article it is said to be in "predicate position."

18. Relative Pronouns

Lesson in a Nutshell

> The relative pronoun ("who," "which") looks like the 2-1-2 noun ending chart. They always have a rough breathing and an accent mark. Relative pronouns introduce relative clauses.

Relative pronouns introduce relative clauses. Here are some examples of relative clauses in English.

The man <u>who is teaching us Greek</u> is bald.

Students <u>who listen well</u> will pass this class.

Joy will fill the hearts of people <u>on whom the Spirit falls</u>.

Is this the book <u>of which you speak</u>?

Do you see how in each case, the underlined clause acts like an adjective to modify a noun?

The "<u>who-is-teaching-us-Greek</u>" man.
The "<u>who-listen-well</u>" students.
The "<u>on-whom-the-Spirit-falls</u>" people.
The "<u>of-which-you-speak</u>" book.

The confusing thing is that in English, the relative pronoun and the interrogative pronoun use the same forms. For example, I might say:

Who is teaching us Greek?
Who is listening well?
On whom does the Spirit fall?

If the pronoun asks a question, it is an interrogative pronoun.

If it connects a relative clause with a noun, it is a relative pronoun.

This is a problem with **English**, not Greek. Greek has different forms for the relative and interrogative pronouns.

Relative: ὅ

Interrogative: τίς

We will meet the interrogative pronoun in our next lesson.

In English, the relative pronoun is "who," "whom," or "which." It does not change form very much.

In Greek, every relative pronoun will give you its case, number and gender. Therefore, there will be more forms.

The relative pronoun is very easy to recognize. It follows a nice 2-1-2 pattern, the one we are growing to love.

The relative pronoun looks very much like the noun endings chart with one important difference. Do you see it?

Relative Pronoun						
		M (2)		F (1)		N (2)
Singular	Nom	ὅς who		ἥ who		ὅ which
	Gen	οὗ of whom		ἧς of whom		οὗ of which
	Dat	ᾧ to whom		ᾗ to whom		ᾧ to which
	Acc	ὅν whom		ἥν whom		ὅ which
Plural	Nom	οἵ who		αἵ who		ἅ which
	Gen	ὧν of whom		ὧν of whom		ὧν of which
	Dat	οἷς to whom		αἷς to whom		οἷς to which
	Acc	οὕς whom		ἅς whom		ἅ which

Noun Endings					
Masculine (2nd declension)		**Feminine** (1st declension)		**Neuter** (2nd declension)	
ος	λογος word	α or η	αρχη beginning	ον	εργον work
ου	λογου of a word	ας or ης	αρχης of a beginning	ου	εργου of work
ῳ	λογῳ to a word	ᾳ or ῃ	αρχῃ to a beginning	ῳ	εργῳ to work
ον	λογον word	αν or ην	αρχην beginning	ον	εργον work
οι	λογοι words	αι	αρχαι beginnings	α	εργα works
ων	λογων of words	ων	αρχων of beginnings	ων	εργων of works
οις	λογοις to words	αις	αρχαις to beginnings	οις	εργοις to works
ους	λογους words	ας	αρχας beginnings	α	εργα works

The relative pronoun will always have **both** a

rough breathing mark
and
an accent.

You will find relative pronouns relatively easy to spot.

Remember: when you see a relative pronoun, look for a relative clause that modifies some noun.

19. Interrogative and Indefinite Pronouns

Lesson in a Nutshell

Interrogative and indefinite pronouns follow the 3-3 pattern and are identical except that the interrogative pronoun always has an accent on the first syllable.

The relative and interrogative pronouns can be confusing because of overlapping forms in Greek and English.

	Relative	Interrogative	Indefinite
English	who, which	who? which? what?	someone something anyone anything
Greek	ὅς, ἥ, ὅ	τίς, τί	τις, τι

Be Brave!

Interrogative and Indefinite Pronouns

Interrogative Pronoun

		M / F (3)		N (3)	
Singular	Nom	τίς	who? what?	τί	which? what?
	Gen	τίνος	of whom? of what?	τίνος	of which? of what?
	Dat	τίνι	to whom? to what?	τίνι	to which? to what?
	Acc	τίνα	whom? what?	τί	which? what?
Plural	Nom	τίνες	who? what?	τίνα	which? what?
	Gen	τίνων	of whom? of what?	τίνων	of which? of what?
	Dat	τίσιν	to whom? to what?	τίσιν	to which? to what?
	Acc	τίνας	whom? what?	τίνα	which? what?

Indefinite Pronoun

		M / F (3)		N (3)	
Singular	Nom	τις	someone something	τι	something
	Gen	τινός	of someone of something	τινός	of something
	Dat	τινί	to someone to something	τινί	to something
	Acc	τινά	someone something	τι	something
Plural	Nom	τινές	someone something	τινά	something
	Gen	τινῶν	of someone of something	τινῶν	of something
	Dat	τισίν	to someone to something	τισίν	to something
	Acc	τινάς	someone something	τινά	something

The interrogative pronoun interrogates. It asks questions. Who? What? Which? Here are a couple of examples in English.

> Who is enjoying learning Greek?

> What would you rather be doing right now?

> Which is your favorite football team?

As we have seen, one obnoxious coincidence of English is that "who" serves as both the relative pronoun (which we studied in the previous lesson) and the interrogative pronoun. Do not let this confuse you.

> Interrogative: Who is working hard?

> Relative: The students, *who are working hard*, will do well.

The indefinite pronoun does not interrogate. It refers to some undefined subject. Here are a couple of English examples:

> Someone will get tired of this lesson before it is over.

> Hand me something to wipe up this mess!

As you can see, these pronouns look very much alike, even though their meaning is quite different. Can you spot the difference between the two forms?

The difference is that

The interrogative pronoun <u>always</u> has an accent on the first syllable.

The indefinite pronoun <u>never</u> has an accent on the first syllable.

I find it helpful to think of the accent on the first syllable as a question mark.

The Grand Confusion

It is easy to see why there is confusion with these pronouns. In English, there is overlap in form between the forms of the relative and interrogative pronouns. In Greek, there is overlap in form between the interrogative and indefinite pronouns.

	Relative	Interrogative	Indefinite
English	who, which	who? which? what?	someone something anyone anything
Greek	ὅς, ἥ, ὅ	τίς, τί	τις, τι

Please remember that Greek *does* give you a clue to distinguish the interrogative pronoun from the indefinite pronoun. I'll say it again:

The interrogative pronoun <u>always</u> has an accent on the first syllable.

The indefinite pronoun <u>never</u> has an accent on the first syllable.

What pattern of declension do these two pronouns follow? Hopefully you can guess!

turn the page for the exciting answer

3-3

Interrogative Pronoun				
		M / F (3)		N (3)
Singular	**Nom**	τίς — who? what?	τί — which? what?
	Gen	τίνος — of whom? of what?	τίνος — of which? of what?
	Dat	τίνι — to whom? to what?	τίνι — to which? to what?
	Acc	τίνα — whom? what?	τί — which? what?
Plural	**Nom**	τίνες — who? what?	τίνα — which? what?
	Gen	τίνων — of whom? of what?	τίνων — of which? of what?
	Dat	τίσιν — to whom? to what?	τίσιν — to which? to what?
	Acc	τίνας — whom? what?	τίνα — which? what?

Indefinite Pronoun					Masc / Fem 3	Neuter 3
		M / F (3)		N (3)		
Singular	**Nom**	τις — someone something	τι — something	ς	–
	Gen	τινός — of someone of something	τινός — of something	ος	ος
	Dat	τινί — to someone to something	τινί — to something	ι	ι
	Acc	τινά — someone something	τι — something	α	–
Plural	**Nom**	τινές — someone something	τινά — something	ες	α
	Gen	τινῶν — of someone of something	τινῶν — of something	ων	ων
	Dat	τισίν — to someone to something	τισίν — to something	σιν	σιν
	Acc	τινάς — someone something	τινά — something	ας	α

Just in case you have forgotten, this means that they follow

> **third** declension in the masculine <u>and</u> feminine, and
> **third** declension in the neuter.

This looks exactly like the third declension portion of our noun endings chart (in yellow).

Study the charts above until you can see how the third declension endings are being added to show you the case, number, and gender of the pronouns.

Notice that the English forms change a little bit to give you information about their case, number and gender. But the Greek forms do it regularly, consistently, and beautifully.

Yay Greek!

20. Demonstrative and Reflexive Pronouns

Lesson in a Nutshell

Near demonstrative pronouns ("this" and "these") look a lot like third person pronouns except they start with a rough breathing or a τ. **Far demonstrative pronouns** ("that" and "those") begin with ἐκειν.

First person **reflexive pronouns** all begin with ἐμαυτ.

Second person **reflexive pronouns** all begin with σεαυτ.

Third person **reflexive pronouns** all begin with ἑαυτ.

Near and Far Demonstrative Pronouns

Here are examples of the <u>near demonstrative pronouns</u> in an English sentence:

> *This is becoming very easy!*
> *Whatever you did for the least of these, you did for Me.*

And here are examples of the <u>far demonstrative pronouns</u>:

> *Are you finished with that?*
> *Those are my favorite jelly beans!*

Notice that in English, the pronoun does not change except to show whether it is singular or plural. The English chart would look like this:

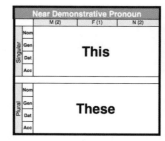 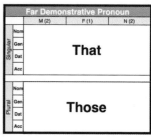

The Greek chart looks like this:

Near Demonstrative Pronoun					
		M (2)		**F (1)**		**N (2)**	
	Nom	οὗτος	this	αὕτη	this	τοῦτο	this
Singular	Gen	τούτου	of this	ταύτης	of this	τούτου	of this
	Dat	τούτῳ	to this	ταύτῃ	to this	τούτῳ	to this
	Acc	τοῦτον	this	ταύτην	this	τοῦτο	this
	Nom	οὗτοι	these	αὗται	these	ταῦτα	these
Plural	Gen	τούτων	of these	τούτων	of these	τούτων	of these
	Dat	τούτοις	to these	ταύταις	to these	τούτοις	to these
	Acc	τούτους	these	ταύτας	these	ταῦτα	these

Far Demonstrative Pronoun					
		M (2)		**F (1)**		**N (2)**	
	Nom	ἐκεῖνος	that	ἐκείνη	that	ἐκεῖνο	that
Singular	Gen	ἐκείνου	of that	ἐκείνης	of that	ἐκείνου	of that
	Dat	ἐκείνῳ	to that	ἐκείνῃ	to that	ἐκείνῳ	to that
	Acc	ἐκεῖνον	that	ἐκείνην	that	ἐκεῖνο	that
	Nom	ἐκεῖνοι	those	ἐκεῖναι	those	ἐκεῖνα	those
Plural	Gen	ἐκείνων	of those	ἐκείνων	of those	ἐκείνων	of those
	Dat	ἐκείνοις	to those	ἐκείναις	to those	ἐκείνοις	to those
	Acc	ἐκείνους	those	ἐκείνας	those	ἐκεῖνα	those

Why is the Greek chart so complicated? Because it gives us the case, number, and gender every time it uses the pronoun.

This is not really complicated. It is just following the 2-1-2 pattern we have grown used to. The way to learn the pronouns is not to memorize every one of them, but to notice the patterns.

The <u>near demonstrative</u> pronouns have either a rough breathing or begin with a τ. Otherwise, they look very much like the third person pronoun.

The <u>far demonstrative</u> pronouns are especially easy to recognize. They always begin with ἐκείν.

Reflexive Pronouns

The reflexive pronouns reflect the action of the verb back onto the subject. For example:

First Person: I plan to read to <u>myself</u> tonight.

Second Person: Give <u>yourself</u> a break!

Third Person: She is very strict with <u>herself</u>.

Here are all of the English forms:

	Singular	Plural
First Person	**myself**	**ourselves**
Second Person	**yourself**	**yourselves**
Third Person	**himself herself itself**	**themselves**

Since Greek gives us the case, number and gender of every substantive, we will expect more forms, but these forms will follow the nice, easy 2-1-2 pattern we already know.

Once you get the hang of a few patterns, Greek is not as hard as it first appears!

Greek Reflexive Pronouns

First Person Reflexive Pronoun

		M (2)	F (1)
Singular	Nom		
	Gen	ἐμαυτοῦ of myself	ἐμαυτῆς of myself
	Dat	ἐμαυτῷ to myself	ἐμαυτῇ to myself
	Acc	ἐμαυτόν myself	ἐμαυτήν myself

Second Person Reflexive Pronoun

		M (2)	F (1)
Singular	Nom		
	Gen	σεαυτοῦ of yourself	σεαυτῆς of yourself
	Dat	σεαυτῷ to yourself	σεαυτῇ to yourself
	Acc	σεαυτόν yourself	σεαυτήν yourself

Third Person Reflexive Pronoun

		M (2)	F (1)	N (2)
Singular	Nom			
	Gen	ἑαυτοῦ of himself	ἑαυτῆς of herself	ἑαυτό of itself
	Dat	ἑαυτῷ to himself	ἑαυτῇ to herself	ἑαυτῷ to itself
	Acc	ἑαυτόν himself	ἑαυτήν herself	ἑαυτό itself
Plural	Nom			
	Gen	ἑαυτῶν of themselves	ἑαυτῶν of themselves	ἑαυτῶν of themselves
	Dat	ἑαυτοῖς to themselves	ἑαυταῖς to themselves	ἑαυτοῖς to themselves
	Acc	ἑαυτούς themselves	ἑαυτάς themselves	ἑαυτα themselves

I did not include the plural forms of the first and second person reflexive pronouns because I ran out of space. But they follow the 2-1-2 pattern. Easy as pie!

You might notice that there are no nominative forms. Why?

Because the reflexive pronoun by definition *receives* the action of the verb. There is no need for a nominative form. For example:

I hit myself.
Myself does not hit myself.

There is really nothing new to learn here except three words. Notice the patterns.

<u>First person</u> reflexive pronouns all begin with ἐμαυτ.

<u>Second person</u> reflexive pronouns all begin with σεαυτ.

<u>Third person</u> reflexive pronouns all begin with ἑαυτ.

Lexical Forms of Pronouns

Pronouns, like the article and adjectives, have forms in all three genders. Therefore, they are listed in their masculine, feminine and neuter forms in the lexicon.

Remember that we are only discussing eleven words. They change form in very regular ways. Once you learn a few patterns you are well on your way to learning Greek!

	Lexical Form	**Pattern**	**Translation**
First Person	ἐγω	no gender	I
Second Person	σύ	no gender	
Third Person	αὐτός, ή, ό	2-1-2	
Relative	ὅς, ἥ, ὅ	2-1-2	Who
Interrogative	τίς, τί	3-3	Who? What? Which?
Indefinite	τις, τι	3-3	someone, something
Near Demonstrative	οὗτος, αὕτη, τοῦτο	2-1-2	this, these
Far Demonstrative	ἐκεῖνος, η, ο	2-1-2	that, those
First Person Reflexive	ἐμαυτοῦ, ῆς, οῦ	2-1-2	of myself
Second Person Reflexive	σεαυτοῦ, ῆς, οῦ	2-1-2	of yourself
Third Person Reflexive	ἑαυτοῦ, ῆς, οῦ	2-1-2	of himself / herself / itself

Valley of the Verbs

Introduction

Welcome to the masterpiece of the Greek language.

We learned that the endings of Greek substantives changed to tell us their case, number and gender.

Greek verbs change form to give us five (!) pieces of information:

tense, voice, mood, person and number.

If you do the math, you quickly discover that the massive number of forms will make you feel like you have landed in Alice's Wonderland.

5 tenses
(present, imperfect, future, aorist, perfect)
X
3 voices
(active, middle, passive)
X
3 moods
(indicative, subjunctive, imperative)
X
3 persons
(first, second, third)
X
2 numbers
(singular, plural)
=
270 forms of every Greek verb![1]

The good news is that just as we saw with substantives, verbs will follow predictable patterns of change. We do not have to learn 270 forms of every verb we meet! We only have to familiarize ourselves with a few regular patterns of variation.

The bad news is that there are more patterns to learn with verbs than with substantives. The verbs can change form so completely that you have no idea what the original was.

Also, we will discover that a few of the commonly used verbs behave with seeming disregard for the rules. Anarchists! But these scofflaw verbs, like all anarchists, follow patterns of their own.

---

[1] This is a rough estimate for demonstration purposes. I have left out the rarely used optative mood and pluperfect tense and am not counting the infinitive as a mood.

21. Tense, Voice, Mood, Person, Number

Lesson in a Nutshell

The goal of this lesson is to understand what tense, voice, mood, person, and number mean.

Every Greek verb will give you five important pieces of information:

1. Tense
2. Voice
3. Mood
4. Person
5. Number

The possibilities are:

Tense	Voice	Mood	Person	Number
Present	**A**ctive	**I**ndicative	**1** First	**S**ingular
Imperfect	**M**iddle	**S**ubjunctive	**2** Second	**P**lural
Future	**P**assive	I**M**perative	**3** Third	
Aorist		(**P**articiple)*		
Pe**R**fect		(I**N**finitive)*		

*technically, not moods, but usually classified here.

In this lesson we will understand what tense, voice, mood, person, and number mean.

Person

We have already discussed the concept of person when we looked at pronouns.

	Singular	Plural
1st Person	"I"	"We"
2nd Person	"You"	"You (all)"
3rd Person	He, She, It	They

Number

Number tells us whether the subject of the verb is singular or plural. No sweat!

Voice

The voice of a verb describes the relationship between the subject of the verb and the action of the verb.

	Meaning	Example
Active	The subject does the action of the verb	I study
Middle	The action of the verb ricochets back to affect the speaker in some way	I study (for myself)
Passive	The subject receives the action of the verb	I am studied

- In the <u>active voice</u> the subject does the action of the verb.

- In the <u>middle voice</u> the subject does the action of the verb and that action comes back to affect the subject in some way. The middle voice is one of the subtleties that was disappearing from the Greek language at the time of the New Testament. There are very few verbs in the New Testament that have a clearly "middle" meaning.

- The <u>passive voice</u> describes the subject receiving the action of the verb.

Mood

The mood of the verb describes the relationship of the verb to reality.

	Meaning	Example
Indicative	The mood of reality	I study.
Subjunctive	The mood of possibility or probability	I might study.
Imperative	The mood of command	Study!

Tense

In English, tense primarily has to do with time — when an action takes place. We speak of past, present, and future tenses.

    Present: I fly
    Future: I will fly
    Past: I flew

Greek tense also gives us information about when the action took place, but it also tells us what *kind* of action took place. "Kind of action" is called "aspect." There are three aspects in Greek. They are often represented with lines and dots.

1. Continuous aspect
   ─────
2. Undefined aspect
   ▪
3. Perfected aspect
   ▪ ─────

- <u>Continuous</u> aspect describes the action as ongoing.

- <u>Undefined</u> aspect just says something took place without giving any information about the kind of action.

- <u>Perfected</u> aspect tells us that an event took place with results that continue.

The chart below illustrates the aspect and time of the five Greek tenses.

NOW	Aspect	Time
Present ——— (▪) ⊞	Continuous (or undefined)	Present
Imperfect ———	Continuous	Past
Future ▪	Undefined	Future
Aorist ▪	Undefined	Past
Perfect ▪——→	Past event with ongoing results	Past to Present

- The <u>present tense</u> describes continuous or undefined action in the present time. (Context will have to be used to determine if the action is continuous or undefined.)

- The <u>imperfect tense</u> describes continuous action in the past time.

- The <u>future tense</u> describes undefined action in the future time.

- The <u>aorist tense</u> describes undefined action in past time. It is the most common way to say that something happened.

- The <u>perfect tense</u> describes an action that took place in the past with continuing results. Exegetically speaking, this is one of the most interesting tenses.

That's it!
On to the wonder of morphology!

22. The Personal Endings

Lesson in a Nutshell

> The personal endings give us four pieces of information about the verb.
>
> 1. The person
> 2. The number
> 3. The voice
> 4. The time of the action
>
> They are very important to learn to recognize!

Obviously, if we set out to study 270 forms of every Greek verb we would soon lose our minds. Instead, we will learn clues to identify the tense, voice, mood, person and number. In most cases, these clues will tell us everything we need to know.

How To Identify Person and Number

Greek (and many other languages) have a very slick way of indicating changes of person and number. Rather than using personal pronouns as we do in English, the ending of the verb is modified in such a way that the person and number are made clear in the verb itself.

Beginning with a simple verb like λύω (I loose), observe how the person and number change as the personal endings change:

Person	Ending	Verb + Ending	Translation
(1s) I	ω	λύω	I loose
(2s) you	εις	λύεις	You loose
(3s) he/she/it	ει	λύει	He/She/It looses
(1p) we	ομεν	λύομεν	We loose
(2p) you (all)	ετε	λύετε	You (all) loose
(3p) they	ουσι(ν)	λύουσιν	They loose

The key to identifying the person and number is to know the personal endings. There are four sets of endings.

Personal Endings			
		Active (do the action)	**Middle/Passive** (receive the action)
Primary (present & future time)	**(1s)** I	ω	ομαι
	(2s) you	εις	η
	(3s) he/she/it	ει	εται
	(1p) we	ομεν	ομεθα
	(2p) you (all)	ετε	εσθε
	(3p) they	ουσι(ν)	ονται
Secondary (past time)	**(1s)** I	ον	ομην
	(2s) you	ες	ου
	(3s) he/she/it	ε(ν)	ετο
	(1p) we	ομεν	ομεθα
	(2p) you (all)	ετε	εσθε
	(3p) they	ον	οντο

Why four? Because these endings do more than tell you person and number. They also give you information about:

1. The **voice** of the verb

> **Active**: The subject does the action of the verb.
> **Middle**: The subject does the action of the verb and it comes back to affect the subject.
> **Passive**: The subject receives the action of the verb.

> Notice the two columns: "Active" and "Middle/Passive."

2. The **time** of the action

> The **primary** endings are used for present and future time.
> The **secondary** endings are used for past time.

> Notice the two rows: "Primary" and "Secondary."

In English, the table would be translated like this

Personal Endings		Active (do the action)	Middle/Passive (receive the action)
Primary (present & future time)	(1s) I / (2s) you / (3s) he/she/it / (1p) we / (2p) you (all) / (3p) they	**I ___** (I jump) I do the action in present time.	**I am ___** (I am jumped) The action is done to me in present time.
Secondary (past time)	(1s) I / (2s) you / (3s) he/she/it / (1p) we / (2p) you (all) / (3p) they	**I ___** (I jumped) I did the action in past time.	**I was ___** (I was jumped) The action was done to me in past time.

The chart below shows the way the endings are applied to λύω and gives the translations.

Personal Endings		Active (do the action)			Middle/Passive (receive the action)		
Primary (present & future time)	(1s) I	λύω	I loose	ω	λύομαι	I am loosed	ομαι
	(2s) you	λύεις	you loose	εις	λύῃ	you are loosed	ῃ
	(3s) he/she/it	λύει	he/she/it looses	ει	λύεται	he/she/it is loosed	εται
	(1p) we	λύομεν	we loose	ομεν	λυόμεθα	we are loosed	ομεθα
	(2p) you (all)	λύετε	you (all) loose	ετε	λύεσθε	you (all) are loosed	εσθε
	(3p) they	λύουσιν	they loose	ουσι(ν)	λύονται	they are loosed	ονται
Secondary (past time)	(1s) I	ἔλυον	I was loosing	ον	ἐλυόμην	I was being loosed	ομην
	(2s) you	ἔλυες	you were loosing	ες	ἐλύου	you were being loosed	ου
	(3s) he/she/it	ἔλυεν	he/she/it was loosing	ε(ν)	ἐλύετο	he/she/it was being loosed	ετο
	(1p) we	ἐλύομεν	we were loosing	ομεν	ἐλυόμεθα	we were being loosed	ομεθα
	(2p) you (all)	ἐλύετε	you (all) were loosing	ετε	ἐλύεσθε	you (all) were being loosed	εσθε
	(3p) they	ἔλυον	they were loosing	ον	ἐλύοντο	they were being loosed	οντο

You may notice something else going on here.

In the secondary row, all of the verbs begin with an ε. Why is that? Because in Greek, when a verb goes into past time, it **augments**. It does this by adding an ε to the front of the verb.

It might help you to think of the way that English puts a verb into the past time.

Jump
becomes
Jumped

The "ed" on the end of the word makes it past time. Think of the ε added to the front of a Greek verb in the same way.

If the Greek verb has an augment on the front, it is in the past time.

So you get two clues you are in the past: the augment and the secondary endings.

Let's experiment with a few examples.

βλέπω means "I see." What would the following forms of βλέπω mean? Cover the answers on the right and see if you can figure out the translations. I will translate them all using the continuous aspect.[1]

βλέπεις	You are seeing
βλέπετε	You (all) are seeing
βλέπομαι	I am being seen
βλέπεσθε	You (all) are being seen
ἔβλεπον	I (or they) were seeing
ἐβλέπομεν	We were seeing
ἐβλέπετο	He/She/It was being seen
ἐβλέποντο	They were being seen

---

[1] The primary forms in these examples are all <u>present</u> tense, which can be undefined or continuous aspect. The secondary forms are all <u>imperfect</u> tense, which can only be continuous aspect. More about this soon.

The hardest part of this **by far** is figuring out the English. Compare the nice compact Greek verbs with the complicated English translations.

Aren't you glad you are learning Greek?

And if you are feeling blown away by all this new information, don't give up! We will be seeing this again and again and again and again…

You will get it!

23. Contract Verbs

Lesson in a Nutshell

Contract verbs are verbs whose stem ends in an α, ε or o. When this happens, the contract vowel and the first vowel of the personal ending change into something new.

As we have seen, Greek modifies verbs by adding letters to the front and back. This creates all kinds of collisions.

Most of the time, no blood is shed. But when certain vowels collide with each other, they morph into something new.

This is a simple chart that accounts for nearly all collisions of vowels.

Vowel Contractions	
οο, οε, εο ➙ ου	εε ➙ ει
any other vowel + ο or ω ➙ ω	αε ➙ α
οη, εοι, οει ➙ οι	εα ➙ η
contract vowel + first vowel of diphthong simplify if the same, otherwise contract	αει ➙ α

Since we do not have to write Greek, only read it, we do not have to become experts at this. We only have to recognize when a collision has happened so it doesn't throw us for a loop.

One of the most common places to see these collisions is with contract verbs. This is a great place to practice on some collisions.

Contract Verbs

Contract verbs are verbs whose stem ends in an α, ε or o. For example:

ἀγαπάω is an α contract verb, meaning "I love"

ποιέω is an ε contract verb, meaning "I do"

πληρόω is an o contract verb, meaning "I fill"

You can easily recognize contract verbs by the vowel before the final omega.

When the personal endings are added to the contract verbs, vowels collide and result in some odd looking personal endings. But there is really nothing odd about it. It is just the normal combination of vowels.

See if you can use the vowel contraction table below to figure out the following collisions. Don't worry about accents.

Vowel Contractions	
οο, οε, εο → ου	εε → ει
any other vowel + ο or ω → ω	αε → α
οη, εοι, οει → οι	εα → η
contract vowel + first vowel of diphthong simplify if the same, otherwise contract	αει → α

Present, Active Contract Verbs

α ἀγαπάω		ε ποιέω		ο πληρόω	
ἀγαπ_____	α ω	ποι_____	ε ω	πληρ_____	ο ω
ἀγαπ_____	α εις	ποι_____	ε εις	πληρ_____	ο εις
ἀγαπ_____	α ει	ποι_____	ε ει	πληρ_____	ο ει
ἀγαπ_____	α ομεν	ποι_____	ε ομεν	πληρ_____	ο ομεν
ἀγαπ_____	α ετε	ποι_____	ε ετε	πληρ_____	ο ετε
ἀγαπ_____	α ουσιν	ποι_____	ε ουσιν	πληρ_____	ο ουσιν

Here are the answers.

ἀγαπάω		ποιέω		πληρόω	
ἀγαπῶ		ποιῶ		πληρῶ	
ἀγαπᾷς		ποιεῖς		πληροῖς	
ἀγαπᾷ		ποιεῖ		πληροῖ	
ἀγαπῶμεν		ποιοῦμεν		πληροῦμεν	
ἀγαπᾶτε		ποιεῖτε		πληροῦτε	
ἀγαπῶσιν		ποιοῦσιν		πληροῦσιν	

Again, you do not have to write Greek, just read it. So if you can just recognize contract verbs, you will be able to understand the strange looking endings.

You do not have to be an expert.
You just have to be able to do two things.

1. Recognize that the strange personal ending is due to the fact that you are dealing with a contract verb.

2. Recognize the shape clearly enough to see which personal ending is being used.

24. Regular Roots & Stems

Lesson in a Nutshell

> Beginning with a root (like λυ), Greek verbs follow a few obvious and consistent patterns to show us their tense.

Let's begin with λύω, a nice, regular verb that plays by all the rules.

On your Master Chart, you will notice that some of the boxes are shaded. These are the oddballs. Never fear! We will master them soon. I have deleted them in the picture below.

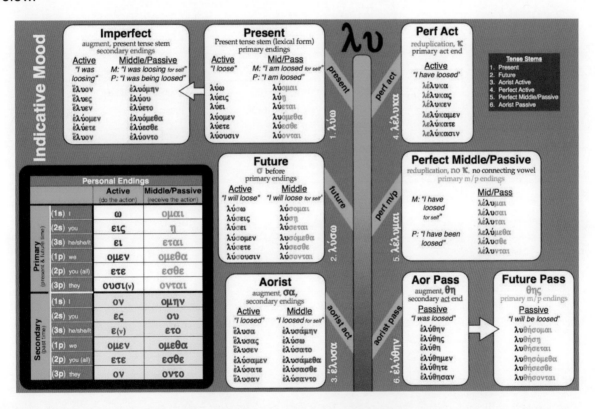

As you can see, there are many forms. But remember: there are only a few patterns.

As we have seen, the personal endings tell us the person and number as well as the voice.

There are only a few clues we need to recognize to determine the tense.

This is the "recipe book" to make all the tenses of λύω. Here is some great news: The clues for λύω hold true for almost all the verbs!

Recipes for Verbs

Tense	Clues	Meaning
Present λύω	Present tense stem (lexical form) primary endings	Ongoing or undefined aspect, present time
Imperfect ἔλυον	augment, present tense stem secondary endings	Ongoing aspect, past time
Future λύσω	σ before primary endings	Undefined aspect, future time
Aorist ἔλυσα	augment, **σα**, secondary endings	Undefined aspect, past time
Perfect Active λέλυκα	reduplication, **κ** primary active endings	Perfected aspect, past to present time
Perfect Middle/Passive λέλυμαι	reduplication, no **κ**, no connecting vowel primary middle/passive endings	Perfected aspect, past to present time
Aorist Passive ἐλύθην	augment, **θη** secondary <u>active</u> endings	Undefined aspect, past time
Future Passive λυθήσομαι	**θης** primary m/p endings	Undefined aspect, future time

Now let's look at these forms, one at a time.

Present (active & middle/passive) Tense

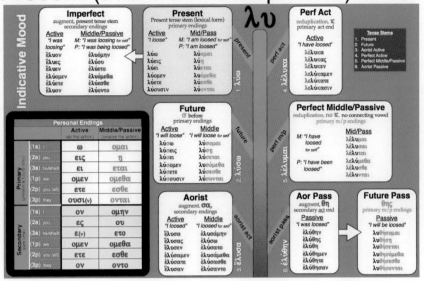

Zoom in!

Personal Endings			Active (do the action)	Middle/Passive (receive the action)
Primary (present & future tense)	(1s) I		ω	ομαι
	(2s) you		εις	η
	(3s) he/she/it		ει	εται
	(1p) we		ομεν	ομεθα
	(2p) you (all)		ετε	εσθε
	(3p) they		ουσι(ν)	ονται
Secondary (past time)	(1s) I		ον	ομην
	(2s) you		ες	ου
	(3s) he/she/it		ε(ν)	ετο
	(1p) we		ομεν	ομεθα
	(2p) you (all)		ετε	εσθε
	(3p) they		ον	οντο

Present
Present tense stem (lexical form)
primary endings

Active "I loose"	Mid/Pass M: "I am loosed for self" P: "I am loosed"
λύω	λύομαι
λύεις	λύη
λύει	λύεται
λύομεν	λυόμεθα
λύετε	λύεσθε
λύουσιν	λύονται

When we learn a verb in Greek we will learn it in the present tense. Because of this, the clue in the present tense is that there is no clue! The present looks just like the lexical form with the primary endings attached.

Imperfect (active and middle/passive) Tense

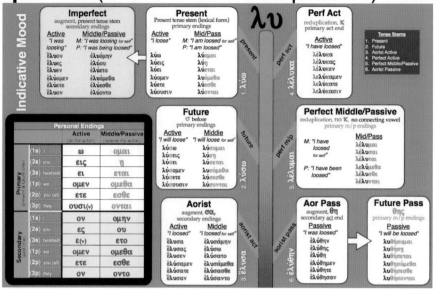

Zoom in!

Personal Endings			Active (do the action)	Middle/Passive (receive the action)
Primary (present & future tense)	(1s) I		ω	ομαι
	(2s) you		εις	η
	(3s) he/she/it		ει	εται
	(1p) we		ομεν	ομεθα
	(2p) you (all)		ετε	εσθε
	(3p) they		ουσι(ν)	ονται
Secondary (past tense)	(1s) I		ον	ομην
	(2s) you		ες	ου
	(3s) he/she/it		ε(ν)	ετο
	(1p) we		ομεν	ομεθα
	(2p) you (all)		ετε	εσθε
	(3p) they		ον	οντο

Imperfect
augment, present tense stem
secondary endings

Active	Middle/Passive
"I was loosing"	M: "I was loosing for self" P: "I was being loosed"
ἔλυον	ἐλυόμην
ἔλυες	ἐλύου
ἔλυεν	ἐλύετο
ἐλύομεν	ἐλυόμεθα
ἐλύετε	ἐλύεσθε
ἔλυον	ἐλύοντο

The imperfect tense is built on the present tense stem.

Since it is in the past time, we attach an augment to the front of the verb and use the secondary endings.

Future (active and middle) Tense

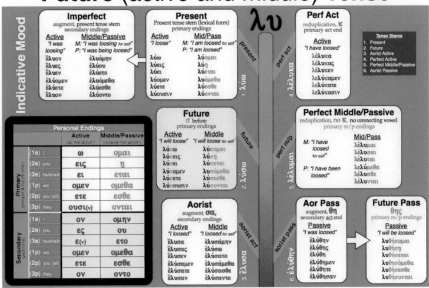

Zoom in!

Personal Endings			Active (do the action)	Middle/Passive (receive the action)
Primary (present & future time)	**(1s)** I		ω	ομαι
	(2s) you		εις	η
	(3s) he/she/it		ει	εται
	(1p) we		ομεν	ομεθα
	(2p) you (all)		ετε	εσθε
	(3p) they		ουσι(ν)	ονται
Secondary (past time)	**(1s)** I		ον	ομην
	(2s) you		ες	ου
	(3s) he/she/it		ε(ν)	ετο
	(1p) we		ομεν	ομεθα
	(2p) you (all)		ετε	εσθε
	(3p) they		ον	οντο

Future
σ before
primary endings

Active "I will loose"	**Middle** "I will loose *for self*"
λύσω	λύσομαι
λύσεις	λύση
λύσει	λύσεται
λύσομεν	λυσόμεθα
λύσετε	λύσεσθε
λύσουσιν	λύσονται

The future is built on the future tense stem. In the case of λύω, it is the same as the present tense stem. As we will see, sometimes it changes a little.

But the big clue for the future is the σ before the primary endings. It is usually very easy to spot.

Aorist (active and middle) Tense

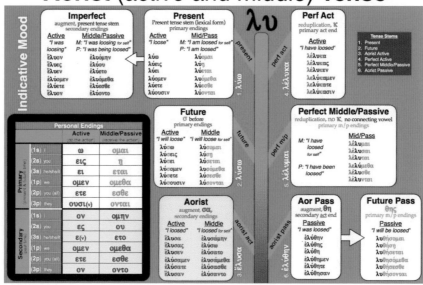

Zoom in!

Personal Endings

		Active (do the action)	Middle/Passive (receive the action)
Primary (present & future tense)	**(1s)** I	ω	ομαι
	(2s) you	εις	η
	(3s) he/she/it	ει	εται
	(1p) we	ομεν	ομεθα
	(2p) you (all)	ετε	εσθε
	(3p) they	ουσι(ν)	ονται
Secondary (past time)	**(1s)** I	ον	ομην
	(2s) you	ες	ου
	(3s) he/she/it	ε(ν)	ετο
	(1p) we	ομεν	ομεθα
	(2p) you (all)	ετε	εσθε
	(3p) they	ον	οντο

Aorist

augment, **σα**,
secondary endings

Active "I loosed"	Middle "I loosed for self"
ἔλυσα	ἐλυσάμην
ἔλυσας	ἐλύσω
ἔλυσεν	ἐλύσατο
ἐλύσαμεν	ἐλυσάμεθα
ἐλύσατε	ἐλύσασθε
ἔλυσαν	ἐλύσαντο

The aorist tense is built on the aorist tense stem. Usually this is easy to spot and looks just like the present with σα attached. Sometimes it is unusual. But more of that later.

Because the aorist tense is undefined action *in the past time*, it uses an augment and the secondary endings, just like the imperfect.

The big clue for the aorist is the σα. As you can see, the σα makes the secondary endings look a little different. Mainly, the connecting vowel gets swallowed up by the α, but the endings are still perfectly recognizable.

Perfect (active) Tense

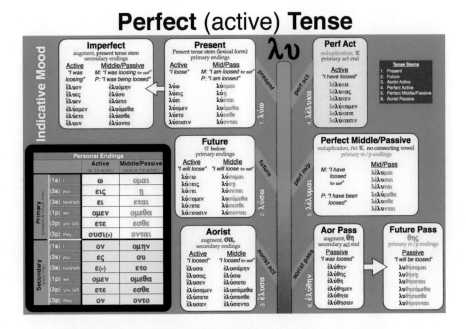

Zoom in!

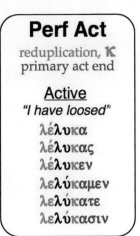

The perfect active is different from the perfect middle/passive, so it gets its own tense stem.

The clues to look for in the perfect active are

> Reduplication[1] on the front of the verb and
> κ before the primary active endings.

As you can see, the endings get swallowed up by the α, just like they did in the aorist and this makes them look somewhat different. But remember: look for *shapes*. Don't insist on exact duplicates.

---

[1] Reduplication means duplicating the first consonant of the word and separating it by an ε. For example, λυ > λελυ

Perfect (middle/passive) Tense

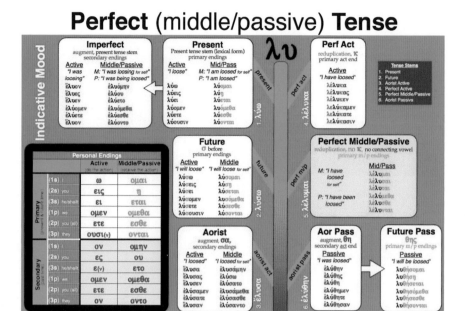

Zoom in!

Personal Endings		Active (do the action)	Middle/Passive (receive the action)
Primary (present & future time)	(1s) I	ω	ομαι
	(2s) you	εις	η
	(3s) he/she/it	ει	εται
	(1p) we	ομεν	ομεθα
	(2p) you (all)	ετε	εσθε
	(3p) they	ουσι(ν)	ονται
Secondary (past time)	(1s) I	ον	ομην
	(2s) you	ες	ου
	(3s) he/she/it	ε(ν)	ετο
	(1p) we	ομεν	ομεθα
	(2p) you (all)	ετε	εσθε
	(3p) they	ον	οντο

Perfect Middle/Passive

reduplication, no **κ**, no connecting vowel
primary m/p endings

M: *"I have loosed for self"*

P: *"I have been loosed"*

Mid/Pass

λέλυμαι
λέλυσαι
λέλυται
λελύμεθα
λέλυσθε
λέλυνται

The perfect middle passive is a bit of an oddball. The forms are not very difficult to recognize.

Because they are perfect, they are reduplicated.

There is <u>no κ</u>. Instead, the primary middle/passive endings are tacked on *without a connecting vowel*. In the second person singular, there is a strange form: σαι. Actually, this is the true form of the second person singular that gets all twisted around in the other forms. Sigmas cause problems for Greek verbs (σαι).

Aorist (passive) Tense

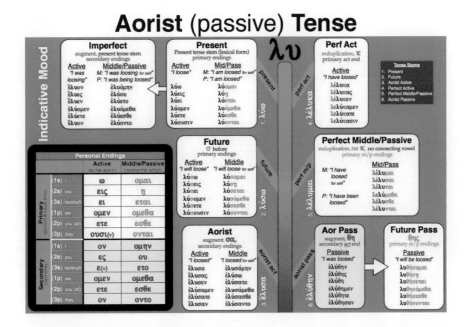

Zoom In!

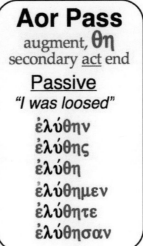

		Active (do the action)	Middle/Passive (receive the action)
Primary (present & future time)	**(1s)** I	ω	ομαι
	(2s) you	εις	η
	(3s) he/she/it	ει	εται
	(1p) we	ομεν	ομεθα
	(2p) you (all)	ετε	εσθε
	(3p) they	ουσι(ν)	ονται
Secondary (past time)	**(1s)** I	ον	ομην
	(2s) you	ες	ου
	(3s) he/she/it	ε(ν)	ετο
	(1p) we	ομεν	ομεθα
	(2p) you (all)	ετε	εσθε
	(3p) they	ον	οντο

The aorist passive gets its own form. It is usually very easy to spot.

Because it is in the past time, it is augmented.

It uses θη to identify itself. This usually sticks out like a sore thumb.

The odd thing about the aorist passive is that it uses secondary *active* endings. (You would expect to use middle/passive endings.) But no big deal. The θη makes it obvious that it is a passive form. And the person and number are easy to spot if you focus on the patterns.

Future (passive) Tense

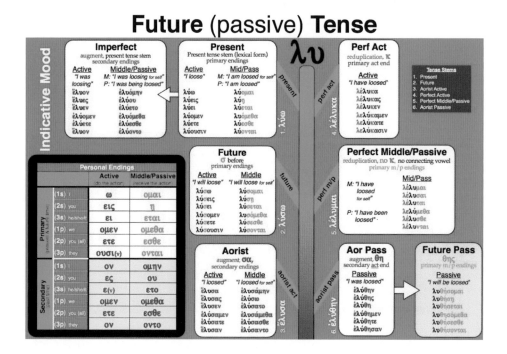

Zoom In!

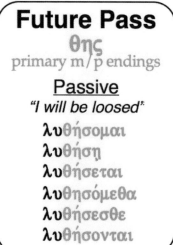

The future passive is sort of an oddball. It is built on the aorist passive tense stem. But it is easy to recognize.

It uses θης to identify itself. We are used to thinking of σ as an identifier for the future.

Plus, we use the primary middle/passive endings, which makes sense.

Actually, even though this is an odd form, it is very easy to recognize. The θης will shout, "Future passive!" to you.

So there you have it. All the forms of λύω!

But here's the deal: If you understand how λύω changes to show you its tense, you are well on your way to understanding Greek verbs, because most of them follow a similar pattern.

One more time. Here is a summary of the clues that will be used to recognize tense. Take some time to make friends with this table!

Tense	Clues
Present λύω	Present tense stem (lexical form) primary endings
Imperfect ἔλυον	augment, present tense stem secondary endings
Future λύσω	σ before primary endings
Aorist ἔλυσα	augment, σα, secondary endings
Perfect Active λέλυκα	reduplication, κ primary active endings
Perfect Middle/Passive λέλυμαι	reduplication, no κ, no connecting vowel primary middle/passive endings
Aorist Passive ἐλύθην	augment, θη secondary <u>active</u> endings
Future Passive λυθήσομαι	θης primary m/p endings

25. Adverbs

Adverbs modify verbs. They do not change form.

What a relief to come across a topic that can be <u>learned</u> as easily as adverbs!

Two factors make Greek adverbs very simple.

1. <u>They do not change form</u>. Yep! You heard me right. They don't morph, decline, shape-shift, or otherwise modify their appearance. Once you learn an adverb, you're through. Yay!

2. There aren't very many of them. Greek uses adverbial participles and adverbial conjunctions to modify verbs. These aren't so easy. But the pure adverbs themselves could not be more simple. In fact, here are all of the adverbs used more than fifty times in the New Testament.

Adverbs

Greek	English	Cognates & Memory Aids
ἀμήν	truly	transliteration of Hebrew exclamation amen
ἐκεῖ	there	
ἔτι	still, yet, even	
εὐθύς	immediately	
ἤδη	now, already	
μή	not	
μηδέ	but not, nor, not even	
νῦν	now	
οὐ, οὐχ, οὐχι	not	
οὕτως	thus	
πάλιν	again	
πῶς	how?	
τότε	then	
ὧδε	here	

In the following English sentences, I have colored the adverb light green and underlined the verb it modifies. See if this makes sense to you.

1. The students <u>studied</u> diligently for the Greek test.

2. They spent three hours busily <u>completing</u> the exam.

3. They <u>were</u> not happy about their grades!

4. The instructor <u>did</u> not prepare them for the test.

5. He <u>did</u> not allow them to take the test again.

6. They <u>went</u> immediately to report him to the Dean.

Please notice that "not" is a very common adverb. It takes the meaning of the verb and turns it into its opposite. In John 1, we will see "not" used repeatedly.

(Did you notice that in the sentence above, that "<u>used</u> repeatedly" is another example of an adverb?)

That's really all there is to adverbs!

The students <u>cheered</u> wildly at the good news!

The Labyrinth

Strange Twists Verbs Take

26. Liquid Verbs

Lesson in a Nutshell

Liquid verbs have stems that end in λ, μ, ν or ρ. When these consonants combine with σ, the sigma drops. This oddity occurs in the future and aorist tense.

A Liquid Form: μένω

Liquid verbs are verbs whose root ends in λ, μ, ν or ρ.

These letters are called "liquids." They are called this because of the way air flows over the tongue (λ and ρ) or through the nose (μ and ν) when they are pronounced. But no need to worry about those details.

For now, it is elementary to remember these four letters. That's:

elementary
or
lmnr_y
if you like.

λ, μ, ν and ρ

The quirk of these letters is that they do not like to be followed by σ, so when a personal ending uses a σ after these letters it simply drops.

QUICK QUIZ

Which tenses use a σ?

(Turn the page for the exciting answer.)

Tense	Clues
Future ´ λυσω	σ before primary endings
Aorist ἔλυσα	augment, σα, secondary endings

So liquid forms affect only the future and aorist tenses.

On your master chart, you will see that I have listed the liquid forms for the verb μένω.

Notice that μένω has a stem that ends in a liquid consonant, ν. We could not use λύω as an example of a liquid verb. Why? Because its stem does not end in a liquid consonant. On all of the shaded verbs on the chart, notice that we had to use a different verb (typed vertically in the bubble). λύω won't work because λύω is perfectly regular.

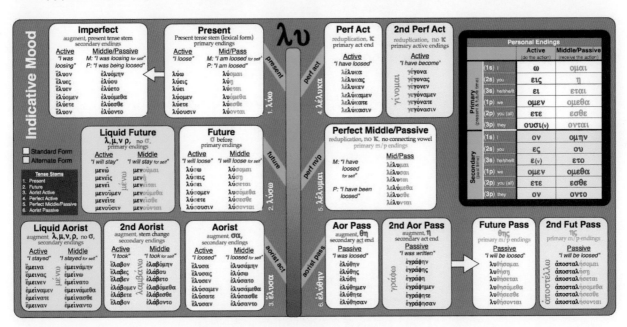

In this chapter, I will give you a detailed explanation for how liquid verbs behave. Please don't get lost in the details. Remember the big picture!

The only thing you need to remember about a liquid verb is that <u>it drops the sigma</u> in the future and aorist tense because <u>σ does not like to follow</u> λ, μ, ν <u>and</u> ρ.

It's **elementary,** remember?

Μένω: **A Sweet Liquid Future**

Let's zoom in and look at μένω, a great example of a liquid future.

If μένω were not a liquid verb, we would expect the future to look like this:

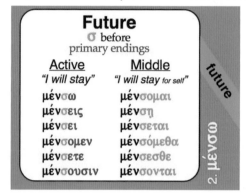

Do you see the problem? In each form we have a liquid (ν) followed by a σ.

But Greeks do not like liquids consonants to be followed by sigmas!

So they drop the sigma. The result looks like this:

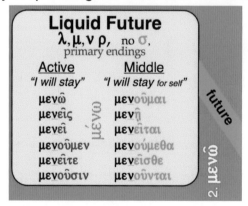

Why the strange augmented vowels with the circumflexes? Here is the full explanation just in case you want to know. (Don't get hung up on it.)

The actual tense formative for liquid futures is not σ but εσ. Here is what happens, taking the first person plural as an example.

μεν + ες + ομεν

becomes

μενεσομεν

But Greeks did not like sigmas to stand between two vowels
(They had issues with sigmas. I think they needed counseling.)

So they dropped the sigma

μενεομεν

Do you remember the vowel contraction chart?
εο becomes ου.

The result is

μενοῦμεν

Too much information? Probably.

You do not need to remember all that. There are only two things you need to remember to identify a liquid future.

1. **After the liquid consonant (λ, μ, ν, or ρ), the sigma is not used.**

2. **The endings of the liquid futures wind up looking just like epsilon contract verbs.**

On the next page,
compare the liquid verb μένω
with the contract verb ποιέω.

μένω	ποιέω
μενῶ	ποιῶ
μενεῖς	ποιεῖς
μενεῖ	ποιεῖ
μενοῦμεν	ποιοῦμεν
μενεῖτε	ποιεῖτε
μενοῦσιν	ποιοῦσιν

How will you be able to tell the liquid futures apart from the epsilon contract verbs?

There are two ways.

1. A liquid consonant will precede the personal ending if it is a liquid future. Notice that this is not the case with ποιέω. λ, μ, ν and ρ are your friends! Learn to spot them!

2. When you learn the verb, you will learn that it is not an epsilon contract. The lexical form is μένω, not μενέω.

Μένω: A Liquid Aorist

Since σα is used in the aorist tense, we have a similar collision between a liquid consonant and a sigma.

We would expect this.

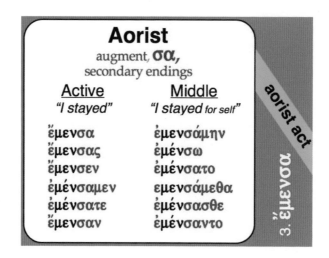

Aorist
augment, **σα,**
secondary endings

Active "I stayed"	Middle "I stayed for self"
ἔμενσα	ἐμενσάμην
ἔμενσας	ἐμένσω
ἔμενσεν	ἐμένσατο
ἐμένσαμεν	ἐμενσάμεθα
ἐμένσατε	ἐμένσασθε
ἔμενσαν	ἐμένσαντο

aorist act

3. ἔμενσα

See the problem?

In each form we have a liquid (ν) followed by a
σ.

But Greeks do not like
liquids to be followed by sigmas!

So they drop the sigma.

So instead, the liquid aorist looks like this.

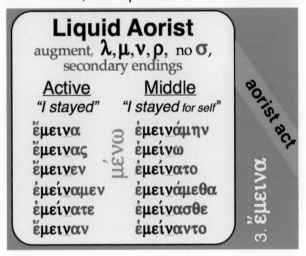

Do you see how the sigma dropped out, leaving just the alpha? In the liquid aorists there are no strange vowel contractions, just a missing sigma.

Instead of
σα
σας
σεν
σαμεν
σατε
σαν

We have
α
ας
εν
αμεν
ατε
α

But there is one other difference that you might notice.

The vowel in μεν became μειν

Why?

Here is an answer you need to get used to:

It just does!

There are many things in language that just happen. I suppose there is a long historical explanation of why. But it is best to just accept it.

As we will see,

Often with the liquid verbs,
there is some sort of vowel change.

No big deal!

We will still be able to recognize them.

Look for basic shapes. Do not insist on exact forms. We are learning to recognize general patterns. This is the key to the Greek verbal system.

To Summarize

Liquid verbs are verbs whose stem ends in a λ, μ, ν, or ρ.

When the sigma of a future or aorist tense formative comes into contact with these letters,

1. The sigma drops.

2. The vowels can do funny things.

That is all there is to the liquid verbs.

27. Second Aorists
Lesson in a Nutshell

Rather than using σα to show that they are aorists, second aorists undergo a stem change. This is not unlike how in English the past tense of "go" is "went."

Rather than using σα to show that they are aorists, second aorists undergo a stem change.

If you understand the previous sentence, you understand second aorists. That's all there is to them.

It is easiest to show what a second aorist is by beginning with English.

In English, we have a regular way to put things in past tense — we add ed.

So, for example:

Today I clean.
Yesterday I cleaned.

Today I play.
Yesterday I played.

But there is another way that English verbs move into past time. They undergo a stem change. For example:

Today I teach.
Yesterday I taught.

Today I go.
Yesterday I went.

Today I run.
Yesterday I ran.

Little kids often say something like this:

Yesterday I goed swimming with my mom. We correct them and say, "Yesterday you went swimming with your mom."

But actually, the kid is applying a logical rule to "go" to make it into "goed." The problem is not with the kid's logic. The problem is with English!

In Greek, second aorists are exactly like this. We have already seen one thing Greek verbs do to show they move into past time — they add an augment to the front of the verb.

But how do Greek verbs normally indicate they are in the aorist tense?

They add σα.

λύω I loose
ἔλυσα I loosed

βλεπω I see
ἔβλεψα[1] I saw

Second aorists do not follow the rules.
They do not add σα.

They undergo a stem change.
Just like in English!

For example:

λάμβανω: I take
ἔλαβον: I took

βάλλω: I throw
ἔβαλον: I threw

Sometimes these changes are very obvious (as in λάμβανω/ἔλαβον.) Other times there is only the difference of a single letter (as in βάλλω/ἔβαλον.)

Which set of endings would you expect the second aorists to use, primary or secondary?

Secondary, of course.
We are in past time.

---

[1] Notice that the σ is "hidden" in the ψ. ἔβλεπσα became ἔβλεψα. See the square of stops.

Without the σα, the endings look much more normal to us. In fact, the second aorists look exactly like imperfects with one important difference:

the stem change

I put that in big, bold blue since it is so important to remember. Second aorists are simply verbs that show you they have moved to the aorist tense by changing their stem rather than adding a σα.

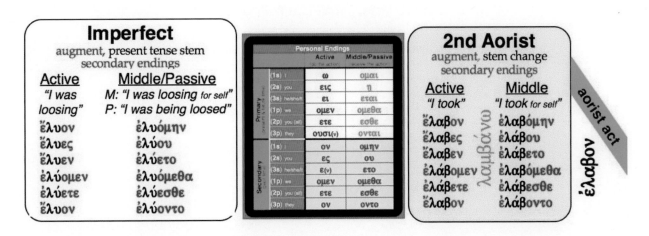

Look at how λαμβάνω shows it is an aorist. No σα. Just the stem change.

Compare the second aorist of λαμβάνω with the imperfect of λύω. Do you see how similar they are?

Here is the second aorist on the Master Chart.

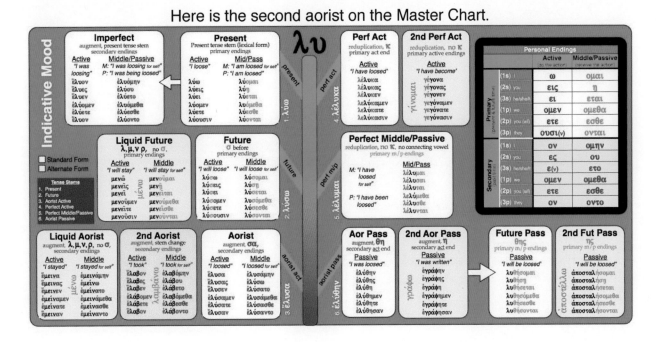

Please notice that there are three types of aorists: Regular, liquid and second.

This has nothing to do with the meaning!

These are just different forms that aorists use to say, "Hey! I'm an aorist!"

One more time: What is a second aorist?

A verb that shows does not use σα to show you it is aorist.
Instead, it uses

a stem change!

That's all there is to it.

28. Deponents

Lesson in a Nutshell

> A deponent verb has an active meaning even though its form is middle or passive.
>
> Verbs that start with vowels augment by lengthening the vowel.

Deponents are weird, but they are not difficult.

If you understand the following sentence, you understand deponents.

Deponents are middle or passive in form
but active in meaning.

Allow me to illustrate.

Consider a very common Greek verb, ἔρχομαι (which means "I come").

The ending is middle/passive, as you realize by now.

Personal Endings		Active (do the action)	Middle/Passive (receive the action)
Primary (present & future time)	(1s) I	ω	ομαι
	(2s) you	εις	η
	(3s) he/she/it	ει	εται
	(1p) we	ομεν	ομεθα
	(2p) you (all)	ετε	εσθε
	(3p) they	ουσι(ν)	ονται
Secondary (past time)	(1s) I	ον	ομην
	(2s) you	ες	ου
	(3s) he/she/it	ε(ν)	ετο
	(1p) we	ομεν	ομεθα
	(2p) you (all)	ετε	εσθε
	(3p) they	ον	οντο

Since ἔρχομαι has a middle/passive ending, you would expect the translation "I am come" or "I am being come" (which doesn't even make sense).

Never fear! The correct translation of ἔρχομαι is "I come."

See? ἔρχομαι is middle/passive in form, but active in meaning.

How will you know if a verb is deponent? Because when you learn the verb, you see that the ending is "ομαι" rather than "ω."

You will learn the word as ἔρχομαι, not ἔρχω. There is no such verb as ἔρχω.

Deponent verbs are easy to spot in the lexicon because they will end in "ομαι" rather than "ω." This is because...

Ἔρχομαι is deponent.
It is middle/passive in form but active in meaning.

Here are thirteen of the most common deponents in Hellenistic Greek. Please notice that four of the thirteen are forms of ἔρχομαι with a preposition attached.

Deponent Verbs (present)		
ἀπέρχομαι	I depart	
ἀποκρίνομαι	I answer	
ἄρχομαι (ἄρχω means "I rule")	I begin	
ἀσπάζομαι	I greet, salute	
γίνομαι	I am, become	
δέχομαι	I receive	
δύναμαι	I am able, powerful	Dynamite gets the job done.
εἰσέρχομαι	I go into	
ἐξέρχομαι	I go out	We go out through the exit.
ἔρχομαι	I come (go)	
κάθημαι	I sit	
προσέρχομαι	I come to	
προσεύχομαι	I pray	

Ἔρχομαι indicates motion. The preposition shows the direction of the motion.

ἀπό means "away from." ἀπέρχομαι means "I depart."

εἰς means "into." εἰσέρχομαι means "I go into."

ἐκ means "from, out of." ἐξέρχομαι means "I go out."

πρός means "towards, with." προσέρχομαι means "I come to."

Verbs that are formed by a preposition plus a verb are called **compound verbs**. They are very common in Greek.

Here are the present and imperfect forms of ἔρχομαι.

Notice again that they are middle/passive in form, but active in meaning.

ἔρχομαι	I come	ἠρχόμην	I was coming
ἔρχῃ	You come	ἤρχου	You were coming
ἔρχεται	He/She/It comes	ἤρχετο	He/She/It was coming
ἐρχόμεθα	We come	ἠρχόμεθα	We were coming
ἔρχεσθε	You (all) come	ἤρχεσθε	You (all) were coming
ἔρχονται	They come	ἤρχοντο	They were coming

That's all there is to deponents.

Deponents are verbs which are middle or passive in form
but active in meaning.

Augmenting on Augments

Verbs That Begin with Vowels

Augmenting a verb is simple if the verb begins with a consonant.

λυ becomes ἐλυ

But what if the verb begins with a vowel, as is the case with ἔρχομαι? If we were to simply add an ε it would look like this.

ἐερχ

You can probably guess by now that the Greeks did not like that barbaric double epsilon. So here's the rule.

If a verb begins with a vowel, it is augmented
by lengthening the vowel.

ἐερχ becomes ἠρχ

Here is another example of augmenting a verb by lengthening a vowel.

Present	Imperfect
ἀγαπῶ I am loving	ἠγαπῶν I was loving

Verbs that begin with prepositions
(compound verbs)

Many Greek verbs begin with a preposition. These are called compound verbs.

Where do you think the augment comes on a verb that begins with a preposition:
- ☐ before the preposition or
- ☐ between the preposition and the verb?

The answer is:

When a verb begins with a preposition,
the augment comes <u>between</u> the preposition and the verb.

Here are some examples:

Present	Aorist
περιπατέω	περιεπάτησα
προσεύχομαι	προσηυξάμην
ἐπερωτάω	ἐπηρώτησα
ἀποστέλλω	ἀπέστειλα

As you can see, the augment between the preposition and verb may do one of a number of things, including

➡ simply add an ε (as in περιεπάτησα)

➡ augment (as in προσηυξάμην and ἐπηρώτησα)

➡ change the vowel (as in ἀπέστειλα)

The trick is to look for some sort of change
after the preposition. If there is one, it's probably an augment.

29. Principal Parts

Lesson in a Nutshell

The principal parts of a verb are the six forms from which all others can be made. They are always listed in this order:

1. Present
2. Future
3. Aorist Active
4. Perfect Active
5. Perfect Middle/Passive
6. Aorist Passive

Remember: All we are doing here is observing the crafty ways that Greek verbs give us their tense, voice, mood, person and number.

We have seen how a regular verb like λύω behaves and how certain combinations of vowels contract (lessons 21-24).

We have also learned about oddballs like

✓ **Liquid futures and aorists**, which drop the sigma after λ, μ, ν, or ρ (lesson 25).

✓ **Second aorists**, which change their stem to show us they are aorists (lesson 26).

✓ **Deponents**, which are middle/passive in form but active in meaning (lesson 27).

enough already!

Every verb seems to have a mind of its own!

How will we keep this all sorted out?

How did you learn the strange quirks of English? By repetition!

Thankfully, in Greek it is not as hard as English. Once we begin reading Greek in earnest, we will learn to see these patterns easily. Context and other clues will help us. Remember, right now we are just laying a foundation.

There is a slick way that each verb can be catalogued that shows us how it behaves in every form.

By learning six forms of any given verb
(called "principal parts")
we will know it inside out.

We already know the principal parts of the verb λύω and have studied the way this marvelously regular verb behaves.

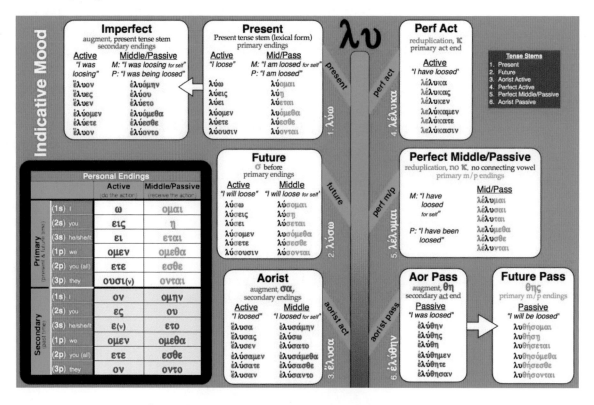

The root of the verb λύω is λυ. Six tense stems branch off from this root.

Observe the vertical words, numbered 1-6. These are the tense stems. They will always be listed in this order.

1. Present
2. Future
3. Aorist Active
4. Perfect Active
5. Perfect Middle/Passive
6. Aorist Passive

λύ

#	Tense Stem	Form	"Recipe"
1	Present	λύω	Present tense stem (lexical form) primary endings
2	Future	λύσω	σ before primary endings
3	Aorist Active	ἔλυσα	augment, σα, secondary endings
4	Perfect Active	λέλυκα	reduplication, κ primary active endings
5	Perfect Middle/Passive	λέλυμαι	reduplication, no κ, no connecting vowel primary middle/passive endings
6	Aorist Passive	ἐλύθην	augment, θη secondary <u>active</u> endings

λύω is our friend because it behaves in a perfectly regular way.

Other verbs do not play so nice — or to be more fair to them,
they follow different rules.

Here are the six principal parts of the verb ἀποστέλλω. Let's take a moment to discuss what is happening in each tense stem.

ἀποστελ

#	Tense Stem	Form	"Recipe"
1	Present	ἀποστέλλω	Present tense stem (lexical form) primary endings
2	Future	ἀποστελῶ	*liquid future* drop the σ after λ, μ ν, ρ primary endings
3	Aorist Active	ἀπέστειλα	*liquid aorist* augment, drop the σ after λ, μ ν, ρ, leaving just α, secondary endings
4	Perfect Active	ἀπέσταλκα	reduplication, κ primary active endings
5	Perfect Middle/ Passive	ἀπέσταλμαι	reduplication, no κ, no connecting vowel primary middle/passive endings
6	Aorist Passive	ἀπεσταλην	*Second Aorist Passive* augment, η secondary <u>active</u> endings

1. The present tense stem adds a λ to the stem. It is normal for the present stem to do odd things. It is actually the least regular.

2. The future tense lacks a σ because of the λ. It is a liquid future.

3. The aorist tense lacks a σ because of the λ. It is a liquid aorist. But where is the augment? It comes between the preposition απο and the verb στελλω (explained in lesson 27).

4. Why the ε? This is the reduplication. Reduplications are added between the preposition and the noun just as augments were. You may have wondered how to reduplicate a verb that starts with a vowel. It would be odd to duplicate the first vowel and separate it with an ε. (αποεοσταλκα). Instead, verbs that begin with vowels do something called a vocalic reduplication. These behave very much like augments.

5. Why the ε? This is the reduplication. (See #4.)

6. This is a second aorist passive. All this means is that there is no θ. Instead, there is only an η.

Here is a picture of ἀποστέλλω and its six stems.

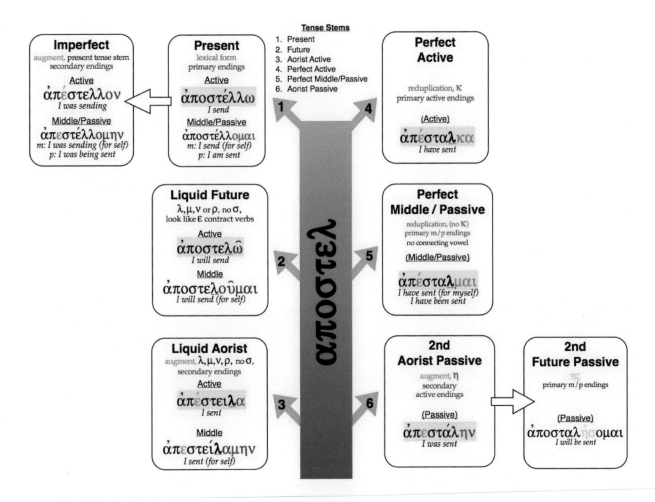

Here are the six principal parts of the second aorist verb βάλλω. (βάλλω is also a liquid future.)

$$βαλ$$

#	Tense Stem	Form	"Recipe"
1	Present	βάλλω	Present tense stem (lexical form) primary endings
2	Future	βαλῶ	*liquid future* drop the σ after λ, μ ν, ρ primary endings
3	Aorist Active	ἔβαλον	*second aorist* augment, stem change, secondary endings
4	Perfect Active	βέβληκα	reduplication, κ primary active endings
5	Perfect Middle/ Passive	βέβλημαι	reduplication, no κ, no connecting vowel primary middle/passive endings
6	Aorist Passive	ἔβληθην	augment, θη secondary <u>active</u> endings

1. The present tense stem adds a λ to the stem. It is normal for the present form to do odd things to the stem. It is actually the least regular stem!

2. The future tense lacks a σ because of the λ. It is a liquid future.

3. Second aorist. In this case, the stem change is very small (drops a λ).

4. Strange in that the α disappears and an η is inserted before the endings. An oddball! But if you remember that the consonants carry the meaning and don't get freaked out about vowels dancing around a bit, you can recognize all the clues and see what is going on. Remember the *shapes*.

5. (same explanation as #4)

6. (same explanation as #5)

Here is a picture of βάλλω and its six stems.

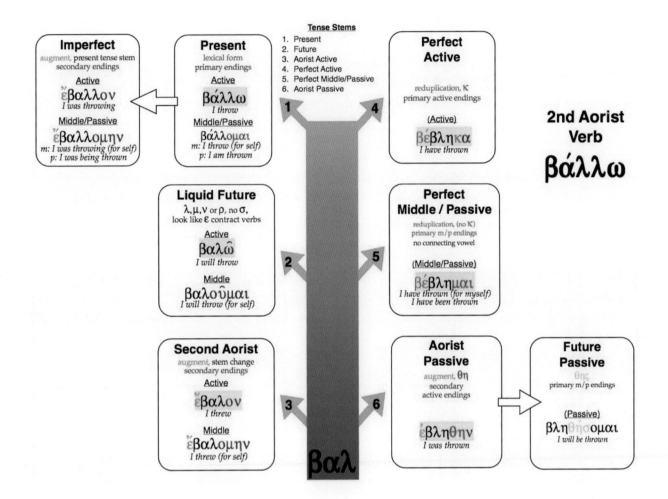

Tense Stems
1. Present
2. Future
3. Aorist Active
4. Perfect Active
5. Perfect Middle/Passive
6. Aorist Passive

Imperfect
augment, present tense stem
secondary endings

Active
ἔβαλλον
I was throwing

Middle/Passive
ἐβαλλομην
m: I was throwing (for self)
p: I was being thrown

Present
lexical form
primary endings

Active
βάλλω
I throw

Middle/Passive
βάλλομαι
m: I throw (for self)
p: I am thrown

Perfect Active
reduplication, κ
primary active endings

(Active)
βέβληκα
I have thrown

2nd Aorist Verb
βάλλω

Liquid Future
λ, μ, ν or ρ, no σ,
look like ε contract verbs

Active
βαλῶ
I will throw

Middle
βαλοῦμαι
I will throw (for self)

Perfect Middle / Passive
reduplication, (no κ)
primary m/p endings
no connecting vowel

(Middle/Passive)
βέβλημαι
I have thrown (for myself)
I have been thrown

Second Aorist
augment, stem change
secondary endings

Active
ἔβαλον
I threw

Middle
ἔβαλομην
I threw (for self)

Aorist Passive
augment, θη
secondary
active endings

ἐβληθην
I was thrown

Future Passive
θης
primary m/p endings

(Passive)
βληθήσομαι
I will be thrown

βαλ

In the Vocabulary Whacker, I have included every verb with its principal parts. Here is an excerpt. Spend some time looking up and down the columns until you can spot the patterns. Don't worry yet about the μί verbs.

Contract Verbs * Second Aorists * Liquid Verbs * Deponents * μι Verbs

Root	Present	Future	Aorist	Perf Act	Perf M/P	Aor Pass
αγαπα	ἀγαπάω I love	ἀγαπήσω	ἠγάπησα	ηγάπηκα	ηγάπημαι	ἀγαπήθην
αγ	ἄγω I lead	ἄξω	ἤγαγον	--	ἦγμαι	ἤχθην
αρ	αἴρω I take up, take away	ἀρῶ	ἦρα	ἦρκα	ἦρμαι	ἤρθην
αιτε	αἰτέω I ask	αἰτήσω	ἤτησα	ἤτηκα	ἤτημαι	--
ακαλουθε	ἀκολουθέω I follow	ἀκολουθήσω	ἠκολούθησα	ἠκολούθηκα	--	--
ακου	ἀκούω I hear	ἀκούσω	ἤκουσα	ἀκήκοα	--	ἠκούσθην
αναβα	ἀναβαίνω I go up	ἀναβήσομαι	ἀνέβην	ἀναβέβηκα	--	--
ανιστα	ἀνίστημι I rise, cause to rise	ἀναστήσω	ἀνέστησα	ἀνέστηκα	ἀνέστημαι	ἀνεστάθην
ανοιγ	ἀνοίγω I open	--	ἀνέῳξα	--	--	ἀνεῴχθην
αποερχ	ἀπέρχομαι I depart	ἀπελεύσομαι	ἀπῆλθον	ἀπελήλυθα	--	--
αποθαν	ἀποθνήσκω I die	ἀποθανοῦμαι	ἀπέθανον	--	--	--
αποκριν	ἀποκρίνομαι I answer	--	ἀπεκρινάμην	--	--	ἀπεκρίθην
αποκτεν	ἀποκτείνω I kill	ἀποκτενῶ	ἀπέκτεινα	--	--	ἀπεκτάνθην

etc!

Go to the Vocabulary Whacker to see the principal parts of every verb used used in the New Testament more than 50 times.

30. μι Verbs, εἰμί

Lesson in a Nutshell

Μι verbs are an ancient form of the Greek verb that behave slightly differently than the others. For the most part, they are very easy to recognize and the clues we have already learned will still apply.

There is one last form of the verb that we must mention. These are usually called the μι verbs because in their lexical form they end in μι in rather than ω.

In John 1 we will come across three μι verbs: δίδωμι, φημί, and ἵστημι.

For study purposes, I have added τίθημι and δείκνυμι to the chart below. The μι verb is an ancient form. There are not very many of them in the New Testament but the few that occur do so with great frequency.

Here are the principal parts of some μι verbs.
What patterns do you see?

Present	Future Active	Aorist Active	Perfect Active	Perfect Middle/ Passive	Aorist Passive
δίδωμι I give	δώσω	ἔδωκα	δέδωκα	δέδομαι	ἐδόθην
ἵστημι I stand	στήσω	ἔστησα	ἕστηκα		ἐστάθην
τίθημι I place, put	θήσω	ἔθηκα	τέθεικα	τέθειμαι	ἐτέθην
δείκνυμι I show	δείξω	ἔδειξα	δέδειχα		ἐδείχθην

For the most part, you would be able to parse the μι verbs just by using the clues you have already learned for the regular verbs. (φημί is an unusual μι verb that only occurs in two tense stems, so don't worry about it.)

Here are the four strange twists that μι verbs throw at you.

1. In the present tense, μι verbs reduplicate the initial letter and separate the reduplicated consonant with an iota.

   This is easy to see with δίδωμι. It is less obvious with the other examples. Here is what happened.

   The root of ἵστημι is στα. When it is reduplicated, it becomes σιστα. But the repetition of the sigma was offensive to the Greek ear, so they turned it into a rough breathing: ἱστα.

   The root of τίθημι is θε. When this is reduplicated it becomes θιθε. You are probably getting enough of a feel for Greek by now to know that this sound would offend the Greek ear. So they de-aspirated the first θ and made it a τ: τιθε.

2. μι verbs use slightly different endings in the present active indicative, as you can see below.

Present Active Indicative
δίδωμι
δίδως
δίδωσιν
δίδομεν
δίδοτε
διδόασιν

3. The stem vowel of the μι verb changes a lot. It can shorten, lengthen, or drop out completely.

4. Most of the μι verbs use κα instead of σα to indicate aorist tense. These are called "kappa aorists."

However, in all the other tenses, the endings look like what we have come to expect. All the clues apply. We simply have to be aware of the slight variations in the present active indicative.

Here is a sample of δίδωμι with endings for your viewing pleasure. Notice how the clues we have learned apply.

Present Indicative	Future Indicative	Aorist Indicative	Perfect Indicative	Present Subjunctive	Aorist Subjunctive
δίδωμι	δώσω	ἔδωκα	δέδωκα	διδῶ	δῶ
δίδως	δώσεις	ἔδωκας	δέδωκας	διδῷς	δῷς
δίδωσιν	δώσει	ἔδωκεν	δέδωκεν	διδῷ	δῷ
δίδομεν	δώσομεν	ἐδώκαμεν	δεδώκαμεν	διδῶμεν	δῶμεν
δίδοτε	δώσετε	ἐδώκατε	δεδώκατε	διδῶτε	δῶτε
δίδόασιν	δώσουσιν	ἔδωκαν	δέδωκαν	διδῶσιν	δῶσιν

εἰμί

εἰμί is a very irregular μί verb. It is also one of the most common words in Greek. The best thing to do is simply memorize it. There is no aorist or perfect form of εἰμί.

εἰμί (I am)			
	Present	Imperfect	Future
1s	εἰμί I am	ἤμην I was	ἔσομαι I will be
2s	εἶ you are	ἦς you were	ἔση you will be
3s	ἐστίν he/she/it is	ἦν he/she/it was	ἔσται he/she/it will be
1p	ἐσμέν we are	ἦμεν we were	ἐσόμεθα we will be
2p	ἐστέ you (all) are	ἦτε you (all) were	ἔσεσθε you (all) will be
3p	εἰσίν they are	ἦσαν they were	ἔσονται they will be

Moody Outlook

The Non-Indicative Moods

31. Subjunctive Mood

Lesson in a Nutshell

The subjunctive mood is the mood of probability, possibility, wishing, etc. It occurs in only two tenses: present and aorist. It is easy to recognize because

1. it is almost always preceded by certain words (especially ἵνα and ἄν).

2. it has a lengthened connecting vowel.

Since outside of the indicative mood, tense no longer indicates time, an augment is not used for the aorist.

So far, we have only encountered the indicative mood. This is <u>by far</u> the most common mood.

Tense	Voice	Mood	Person	Number
Present	**A**ctive	**I**ndicative	**1** First	**S**ingular
Imperfect	**M**iddle	**S**ubjunctive	**2** Second	**P**lural
Future	**P**assive	I**M**perative	**3** Third	
Aorist		(**P**articiple)*		
Pe**R**fect		(I**N**finitive)*		

In the next two lessons, we will conquer the subjunctive mood (chapter 31) and the imperative mood (chapter 32).

You will find these on your Master Chart underneath the indicative mood.

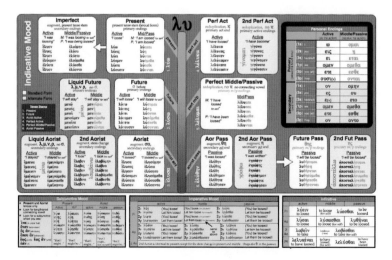

As we have learned, the indicative is the mood used to portray <u>reality</u>. It makes statements and asks questions.

> I am hungry!
>
> I will eat dinner after I finish this lesson.
>
> Does anyone know in which drawer the knives are?

The subjunctive mood is used for <u>possibility</u> or <u>probability</u>.

> <u>If I were</u> finished, I would eat.
>
> I am hurrying <u>in order that I might</u> barbecue some hamburgers.

The subjunctive mood has three nice features that make it very easy to spot.

> 1. Subjunctives only use two tenses.
>
> 2. The endings of subjunctives are simple.
>
> 3. Context almost always tells you when to expect a subjunctive.

Let's look at these one at a time.

Subjunctive Mood					
★ **Present** and **Aorist** tenses only	Present		Aorist		
★ Look for lengthened connecting vowel	Active	M/P	active	middle	passive
★ Look for a subjunctive when you see: ἵνα (in order that) ὅταν (whenever) ὅς ἄν (whoever) ὅπου ἄν (wherever) ἕως (until) ἕως ἄν (until) ἐάν (if)	λύω λύῃς λύῃ λύωμεν λύητε λύωσιν "that I might..."	λύωμαι λύῃ λύηται λυώμεθα λύησθε λύωνται "that I might be..."	λύσω λύσῃς λύσῃ λύσωμεν λύσητε λύσωσιν "that I might..."	λύσωμαι λύσῃ λύσηται λυσώμεθα λύσησθε λύσωνται "that I might... (for myself)"	λυθῶ λυθῇς λυθῇ λυθῶμεν λυθῆτε λυθῶσιν "that I might be..."

1. Subjunctives only use two tenses

In the indicative mood, Greek tense tells us aspect + time.

But outside of the indicative mood, time is not a factor.

Mood / Part of Speech	Tense Describes...
Indicative Mood	Aspect + Time
Subjunctive Mood **Imperative Mood** **Infinitives** **Participles**	Aspect Only

Remember that Greek has three possible aspects:

1. Continuous aspect

2. Undefined aspect

3. Perfected aspect

The subjunctive only occurs in the present and aorist tenses.

Ongoing aspect is captured by the present tense.

Undefined aspect is captured by the aorist tense.

This is why...

The subjunctive mood is found in the
Present Tense
and
Aorist Tense
only!

There is no need for a "future subjunctive" since the subjunctive mood has nothing to do with time.

There is no need for an "imperfect subjunctive" since the present tense already captures the ongoing aspect and there is no need for a "past time" version. The subjunctive mood has nothing to do with time, only aspect.

2. The endings of subjunctives are simple

Present		Aorist		
Active	M/P	active	middle	passive
λύω	λύωμαι	λύσω	λύσωμαι	λυθῶ
λύῃς	λύῃ	λύσῃς	λύσῃ	λυθῇς
λύῃ	λύηται	λύσῃ	λύσηται	λυθῇ
λύωμεν	λυώμεθα	λύσωμεν	λυσώμεθα	λυθῶμεν
λύητε	λύησθε	λύσητε	λύσησθε	λυθῆτε
λύωσιν	λύωνται	λύσωσιν	λύσωνται	λυθῶσιν
"that I might..."	"that I might be..."	"that I might..."	"that I might... (for myself)"	"that I might be..."

Take a look at the endings of the subjunctive. What patterns do you see?

1. Notice the lengthened connecting vowel. In every case, it is either an η or an ω.

2. No tricks at all with the present subjunctive. Use the present tense stem and attach the primary endings (with the lengthened connecting vowels).

3. The aorist uses σα but the α gets swallowed up by the big fat connecting vowel. All that is left is the σ.

4. The aorist subjunctive is not augmented. This may throw you at first. We are used to the aorist being augmented. If you think about it, I'll bet you can figure out why this is the case.

   • What is the augment used for? … To tell you we are in the past time.

   • But in the subjunctive mood, tense does not tell us about time, only aspect. Therefore we do not need an augment.

This leaves the aorist subjunctive looking very much like a future. There is no augment and no σα (since the α was swallowed by the lengthened connecting vowel). But there is no such thing as a future subjunctive!

3. Context almost always tells you when to expect a subjunctive

Even if you miss all of the other clues, context will still make a subjunctive very hard to overlook. There are certain key words that are nearly always followed by a subjunctive.

If you see...	Look for a subjunctive!
ἵνα	*in order that...*
ἐάν	*if...*
ὅταν	*whenever...*
ὅς ἄν	*whoever...*
ὅπου ἄν	*whereever...*
ἕως, ἕως ἄν	*until...*

Do you see how ἄν is used in most of the clues? When we learned ἄν, we learned that it was an untranslatable particle used to make definite things contingent.

ἄν	untranslatable particle used to make definite things contingent

In other words, ἄν introduces uncertainty and uncertainty calls for the subjunctive mood.

A few other things about the subjunctive

1. Did you notice that there are two words used to negate things in Greek, ου and μη? Ου is used to negate the indicative. Μη is used to negate everything else.

2. The most emphatic way to negate something in Greek is to use ου + μη + the aorist subjunctive. It's like negating the possibility of the possibility!

$$\text{κἀγὼ δίδωμι αὐτοῖς ζωὴν αἰώνιον,}$$
and I am giving to them life eternal

$$\text{καὶ οὐ μὴ ἀπόλωνται εἰς τὸν αἰῶνα}$$
and not not they shall perish forever

3. The first person subjunctive may be used to exhort. This is called a "hortatory subjunctive."

εἶπεν ὁ θεός Ποιήσωμεν ἄνθρωπον
said   *   God   "Let us make"   man...

ἀναβῶμεν εἰς Βαιθηλ
"Let us go up" into   Bethel

4. If a question is asked to which the answer is uncertain, the subjunctive may be used. This is called a deliberative subjunctive.

Τί φάγωμεν;   Τί πίωμεν;
What   shall we eat?   What shall we drink?

32. Imperative Mood

Lesson in a Nutshell

The imperative mood is the mood of command. Like the subjunctive mood, it is found only in the present and aorist tenses. Unlike English, Greek has a third person imperative and the ability to indicate ongoing aspect when it makes a command.

The imperative mood is the mood used for commands. It is much the same in Greek as it is in English. However, Greek has two nice additions.

Addition #1
The Third Person Imperative

In English, the implied subject of the imperative is always second person: you!

If I say...

Listen up!
or
Quit slouching!

You assume that I mean

(you) Listen up!
or
(you) Quit slouching!

But Greek has a second AND a third person imperative. There is no great way to translate a third person imperative. The best way to explain the third person imperative is by an example.

One of the things Jesus sometimes said to the crowds was,

ὁ ἔχων[1] ὦτα ἀκουέτω.
The one having   ears   let him hear!

---

[1] This is a participle. We will understand it very soon!

ἀκουέτω is the third person imperative. Do you see how him/her/it is being commanded? We translate it with "let him/her _____." But this is a pale substitution for the Greek imperative. The Greek is stronger. It means something more like:

The one having ears…. HEAR!

Addition #2
Continuous Aspect

Remember that as soon as we leave the indicative mood, time is no longer a factor.

As we saw with the subjunctive mood, there are two aspects that can be captured with the present and aorist tenses.

> Ongoing aspect is captured by the present tense.

> Undefined aspect is captured by the aorist tense.

These are the two tenses used by the imperative mood as well. In other words….

The imperative mood is found in the
Present Tense
and
Aorist Tense
only![1]

In English, the imperative is always undefined. If I tell you to study or to mow the lawn, the aspect is undefined. I am not telling you anything about the *kind* of action involved.

But Greek gives the option of the present tense, which communicates an ongoing state of affairs.

There is a great example of this in John 8. Jesus has just forgiven a woman caught in the act of adultery. Having forgiven her, he issues an imperative.

$$πορεύου \quad καὶ \quad μηκέτι \quad ἁμάρτανε.$$
Go · · · · and · · · no longer · · · · sin.

---

[1] There actually is a perfect imperative, but it is rare (only four in the entire New Testament).

We translate this, "Go and sin no more." But both πορεύου and ἁμάρτανε are present tense. Jesus is commanding an ongoing state of life, not just making an undefined statement. This nuance is lost in English and almost impossible to translate without awkwardness.

The Forms

With the subjunctive mood, we found that the forms were easy and that there were lots of clues to help us spot them.

The same is true of the imperative. Context will help you to expect an imperative.

Even better, the endings never change.

Imperative Mood					
	active		middle		passive
Pr	2s λῦε — (You) loose!		(You) loose (for yourself)!	2s λύου — (You) be loosed!	
	3s λυέτω — Let him loose!		Let him loose (for himself)!	3s λυέσθω — Let him be loosed!	
	2p λύετε — (You) loose!		(You) loose (for yourself)!	2p λύεσθε — (You) be loosed!	
	3p λυέτωσαν — Let them loose!		Let them loose (for themselves)!	3p λυέσθωσαν — Let them be loosed!	
Ao	2s λῦσον — (You) loose!		2s λῦσαι	2s λύθητι — (You) be loosed!	
	3s λυσάτω — Let him loose!		3s λυσάσθω — same as above	3s λυθήτω — Let him be loosed!	
	2p λύσατε — (You) loose!		2p λύσασθε	2p λύθητε — (You) be loosed!	
	3p λυσάτωσαν — Let them loose!		3p λυσάσθωσαν	3p λυθήτωσαν — Let them be loosed!	
2 Ao	Second Aorist is identical to present except for the stem change.				

In the
third person singular
second person plural, and
third person plural,
the endings are always...

τω

τε

τωσαν
in the active voice, and

σθω

σθε

σθωσαν
in the middle or passive voice.

Nice, huh? As you would expect, there is a σα or θη in the aorist.

As you might also expect, there is no augment in the aorist, since outside of the indicative, tense has nothing to do with time.
The only trick is to learn the second person singular endings (in blue). These are fairly common, so do your best to lodge them in your brain.

As usual, a second aorist will not tell you it is an aorist by using σα. Instead, it will undergo a stem change. But that is old news to you by now!

33. Infinitives

Lesson in a Nutshell

Infinitives are the "to-be" verbs. They are easy to recognize but they can be challenging to translate since they are sometimes used in ways that are not like English. Infinitives do not have person and number. They may be present, aorist, or perfect tense.

To be or not to be. That is the question.

Infinitives are the "to be" verbs.

To run, to dance, to sing, to swim, to learn,

to be or not to be.

Infinitives are verbal nouns. They can function just like nouns in a sentence.

To finish this class will be a great relief.
I like to dance but my wife won't let me because I look goofy.

In both cases, the infinitive is behaving like a noun in the sentence, even though it is a verbal idea, hence the designation "verbal noun."

Infinitives are simple because *they do not have person and number*, only tense and voice.

As you might guess by now, the tense of infinitives has nothing to do with time, only aspect. Infinitives come in three tenses, which capture the three Greek aspects.

Present Infinitives
describe ongoing aspect.

─────────────

Aorist Infinitives
describe undefined aspect.

·

Perfect Infinitives
describe perfected aspect.

· ─────────────

Since infinitives lack person and number and are found in only three tenses, there are very few forms.

Infinitive			
	active	**middle**	**passive**
Pr	λύειν to loose	λύεσθαι to loose (for self)	λύεσθαι to be loosed
Ao	λῦσαι to loose	λύσασθαι to loose (for self)	λυθῆναι to be loosed
2 Ao	λαβεῖν to take	λαμβανω (I take) λαβέσθαι to take (for self)	
Pf	λελυκέναι to have loosed	to have loosed (for self) λελύσθαι	to have been loosed

Forms

Present Tense
As usual, the clue for the aorist is that there is no clue. The lexical form will pop out at you.

Aorist Tense
The Aorist infinitive has our old friend σα (active and middle) and θη (passive).

Second Aorist
The second aorist endings are exactly like the present tense. The only difference will be the stem change.

Perfect Tense
The perfect tense will be reduplicated. In the active there will be a κ. In the middle/passive there will be no connecting vowel.

Infinitives are easy to spot. Notice that the present active and second aorist active end in ειν. All other forms end in αι.

As we saw with the subjunctive and imperative, the aspect of the Greek infinitive is very difficult to capture in English. The present and aorist translation, for example, is identical: "to loose." But they mean something different. The aorist describes undefined aspect. The present describes ongoing aspect.

You could translate the present "to continue loosing" but that is pretty clumsy English! Better just to learn Greek.

Translation

Often, the Greek infinitive behaves exactly like the English infinitive and is very easy to translate. Here are a couple of examples.

δύναται ὁ θεὸς ἐκ τῶν λίθων τούτων ἐγεῖραι τέκνα τῷ Ἀβραάμ.
He is able   *   God from   *   stones   these   **to raise** children to   Abraham.

πάντας ἀνθρώπους θέλει σωθῆναι καὶ εἰς ἐπίγνωσιν ἀληθείας
all   people   He wishes **to be saved** and into   knowledge   of truth

ἐλθεῖν.
to come.[1]

The Greek infinitive can also behave in ways that are not like English at all. This takes some getting used to. Do not panic! We will get used to these as we begin to read more Greek.

1. Sometimes the Greek infinitive has the article.

Since the infinitive is a verbal noun, this makes sense. When the infinitive has the article <u>the article will always be singular, neuter</u>. Its case will be determined by the role the infinitive plays in the sentence.

Here is an example.

ἐμοὶ γὰρ τὸ ζῆν[2] Χριστὸς καὶ τὸ ἀποθανεῖν κέρδος.
to me for   **to live** (is) Christ   and   **to die**   (is) gain.

Notice that the article defines the "case" of the infinitive in the sentence. In this example it would be nominative.

---

[1] Notice the shift between the first (σωθῆναι) and second (ἐλθεῖν) aorist.

[2] Remember that ζάω is a contract verb. ζα + ειν contracts to ζῆν.

2. Sometimes the Greek infinitive is used with an article and a preposition to mean something you would never guess.

This usage is called "idiomatic" which means there is no clear way to draw a path between the original Greek and the English translation. You have to know what it means in Greek, then step back and say it in English.

This chart (found on page 8 of your master chart) summarizes these usages.

Prepositions with Infinitives
εἰς τό = *in order that*
μετὰ τό = *after*
διὰ τό = *because*
ἐν τῷ = *when/while*
πρὸ τοῦ = *before*
πρὸς τό = *in order that*

The easiest way to begin to grasp this is to take some examples.

εἰς τὸ βλέπειν αὐτόν
into the   to see   him

A literal transliteration makes no sense at all. This construction has to be recognized. The correct translation of εἰς τὸ βλέπειν αὐτόν is:

In order that he sees.

Huh?? Yep. That's it. In order to translate this idiom, you have to recognize the preposition with the infinitive and see it like this:

εἰς τὸ means "in order that.
βλέπειν means "sees."
αὐτόν means "he" (the "subject" of the infinitive).

The strangest part of this construction is that the subject of the preposition will be in the accusative case but will be translated as if it were in the nominative.

This is tricky since we have trained ourselves to expect accusatives to receive the action of the verb. In this construction they produce the action.

Here are two examples of each construction. Please don't worry and have nightmares about this. Just look these examples over and try to get a feel for this idiomatic use of the infinitive.

εἰς τό _____
in order that

εἰς τὸ πιστεύειν αὐτόν
= in order that he believes

ὁ υἱὸς τοῦ ἀνθρώπου παραδίδοται εἰς τὸ σταυρωθῆναι.[1]
The Son   *   of Man   is handed over   in order to be crucified.

μετὰ τό _____
after

μετὰ τὸ πιστεύειν αὐτόν
= after he believes

μετὰ τὸ ἀποθανεῖν τὸν πατέρα
= after the father dies

διὰ τό _____
because

διὰ τὸ πιστεύειν αὐτόν
= because he believes

διὰ τὸ εἶναι αὐτὸν ἐξ οἴκου καὶ πατριᾶς Δαυίδ
= because he was of the house and family of David.

---

[1] In this instance there is no expressed "subject" of the infinitive. The subject is obviously the Son of Man.

ἐν τῷ _____
when/while

ἐν τῷ πιστεύειν αὐτόν
= while he believes

ἐν τῷ σπείρειν[1] αὐτὸν
= while he sows

πρὸ τοῦ _____
before

πρὸ τοῦ πιστεύειν αὐτόν
= before he believes

τὸ πάσχα φαγεῖν μεθ᾽ ὑμῶν πρὸ τοῦ με παθεῖν[2]
the Passover   to eat   with   you   before I suffer

_____ = to eat the Passover with you before I suffer

πρὸς τό _____
in order that

πρὸς τὸ πιστεύειν αὐτόν
= in order that he believes

πρὸς τὸ δύνασθαι ὑμᾶς στῆναι
= in order that you are able to stand

---

[1] σπείρω = I sow

[2] πάσχω = I suffer

Participle Panorama

Participles

34. Participles Overview

Lesson in a Nutshell

Participles are verbal adjectives, usually translated as "ing" words.

As verbs, they have tense and voice. As adjectives they have case, number and gender.

Participles can behave like adjectives or adverbs.

Ah, the participle,
that wonder of Greek morphology!

The Greek participle will bring together what we have learned about substantives and motion words into one glorious (terrifying?) part of speech.

The good news is that if you have learned the material we have covered so far, there is very little new to learn.

The bad news is that if you have not learned the material we have covered so far, it will come back to haunt you.

The good news is that the participles give us a chance to summarize and review all we have learned so far. Onward!

In this lesson, we will focus on understanding the grammar of the participle — how it behaves in a sentence. I will also introduce you to the basic forms of the Greek participle.

In the three lessons that follow, we will put the participle into play — and play!

What Is A Participle?

A participle is a verbal adjective. It has

➡ some things in common with verbs and
➡ other things in common with adjectives.

In English, the participles are the "ing" words.[1]

flying
running
falling
laughing

Sometimes participles behave like <u>adjectives</u>.
Other times they behave like <u>adverbs</u>.

As adjectives...

Participles can modify nouns — just like adjectives. This is called the adjectival use. Pretty tricky, right?

Here is an example of an <u>adjectival participle</u>.

The hunting dog.

See? "Hunting" modifies "dog."

Participles can also "stand in" for nouns — just like any adjective.

This is called the <u>substantival use</u>.

Hunting is my favorite activity.

In this case "hunting" is behaving like a noun.

As adverbs...

Participles can also modify verbs. In other words, they behave adverbially. This is called the adverbial use of the participle. Who would have guessed?

Here is an example of the adverbial use of the participle.

My dog broke its leg while hunting.

In this case "while hunting" modifies "broke." In other words, the leg "broke while hunting." When the participle is used this way in Greek, it will often require a key word to complete the meaning.

---

[1] Actually, "ing" is used to form the active participle in English and "ed" is used to form the passive participle.

To review: There are three ways the participle is used:

Adjectival
The hunting dog.

Substantival
Hunting is my favorite activity.

Adverbial
My dog broke its leg while hunting.

One more thing...

The participle can stand at the head of a phrase. This is called a participial phrase.

Watch how the participles in our three simple examples can be expanded into participial phrases.

Adjectival
The dog hunting by my side.

Substantival
Hunting with my friends on a cool fall morning is my favorite activity.

Adverbial
The dog broke its leg while hunting in the woods.

As we begin to translate Greek, you will discover that it is very important to see participial phrases.

It's a participle paradise!

Recognizing Greek Participles

Greek participles have tense and voice, case, number and gender.

Tense	Voice	Participle	Case	Number	Gender
Present **A**orist Pe**R**fect	**A**ctive **M**iddle **P**assive	**P**articiple	**N**ominative **G**enitive **D**ative **A**ccusative	**S**ingular **P**lural	**M**asculine **F**eminine **N**euter

Tense: The tense of a participle is not focused on time, but aspect. Remember: everything outside of the indicative is not focused on time.

Participles do have something called "relative time." It means that the action described in the participle takes place relative to the main verb. More about that later.

For now, it is enough to focus on aspect, which is much more important.

It's the same old story:

Present Participles
describe ongoing aspect.

_____

Aorist Participles
describe undefined aspect.

.

Perfect Participles
describe perfected aspect.

. _____

Voice: The voice of the participle tells whether the subject of the participle is giving (active) or receiving (passive) the action of the participle. No surprise there!

Case, Number, Gender: The case, number and gender of the participle will match the noun it modifies. Just as adjectives had to be able to be masculine AND feminine AND neuter, participles must be able to be all three genders. For this reason, there are 24 forms of each participle.

This is not like English, but by now we should be used to it.

There is only one form of the English definite article ("the") but there are 24 forms in Greek. Why? Because every Greek article matches the noun it modifies in case, number and gender. But this is old news.

Because the participle is a verbal adjective, it has 24 forms. It will follow either the 2-1-2 or 3-1-3 pattern of declension. In English, I use the same word whether I am speaking of...

a believing man
believing men
a believing woman
believing women
believing crowds

In Greek, the participle will change to match the case, number and gender of the noun it modifies.

πιστευων[1]   ἀνθρωπος

πιστευοντες   ἀνθρωποι

πιστευουσα   γυνη

πιστευουσαι   γυναικες

πιστευοντες   ὀχλοι

One more time: Participles have tense and voice, case, number and gender.

Tense	Voice	Participle	Case	Number	Gender
Present **A**orist Pe**R**fect	**A**ctive **M**iddle **P**assive	**P**article	**N**ominative **G**enitive **D**ative **A**ccusative	**S**ingular **P**lural	**M**asculine **F**eminine **N**euter

---

[1] The nominative, masculine, singular form of the participle is odd. We have seen this pattern. Nominative forms tend to do their own thing.

We will study the forms in the next three lessons, but the good news is that there is almost nothing new to learn.

* **The present tense** will be built on the present tense stem.
  (It will look like the lexical form.)

* **The Aorist tense** will reveal itself by a σα, θε[1] or a stem change.
  There will be no augment.

* **The perfect tense** will use a reduplication, κ, or no connecting vowel.

* **The voice** of the participle will be easy to see by the participle morpheme.
  (More on that to come.)

Active	Middle or Passive
ντ, ουσα/η ντ, σασα/η κοτ, κυια	μεν, θε

* **The case, number and gender** will be shown by noun endings we have already learned.

---

[1] Instead of a θη the participle uses θε.

35. Present Participles

Lesson in a Nutshell

Present participles are based on the present tense stem.

- Active voice will contain ντ or ουσα. They follow the 3-1-3 pattern.
- Middle/passive voice will contain μεν. They follow the 2-1-2 pattern.

Present participles convey ongoing aspect.

In this chapter, we will learn how to recognize and translate present participles. Let's begin with recognition.

How To Parse a Present Participle

Present Participles					
active ντ, ουσα, ντ 3-1-3			middle/ passive μενο, μενη, μενο 2-1-2		
M (3)	F (1)	N (3)	M (2)	F (1)	N (2)
λύων	λύουσα	λῦον	λυόμενος	λυομένη	λυόμενον
λύοντος	λυούσης	λύοντος	λυομένου	λυομένης	λυομένου
λύοντι	λυούσῃ	λύοντι	λυομένῳ	λυομένη	λυομένῳ
λύοντα	λύουσαν	λῦον	λυόμενον	λυομένην	λυόμενον
λύοντες	λύουσαι	λύοντα	λυόμενοι	λυόμεναι	λυόμενα
λυόντων	λυουσῶν	λυόντων	λυομένων	λυομένων	λυομένων
λύουσιν	λυούσαις	λύουσιν	λυομένοις	λυομέναις	λυομένοις
λύοντας	λύουσας	λύοντα	λυομένους	λυομένας	λυόμενα

I know that when you first look at this table it makes you want to run for the hills screaming.

There is no need for such drastic measures!

You already know everything!

Tense and voice, case, number and gender, remember?

Tense	Voice	Participle	Case	Number	Gender
Present **A**orist Pe**R**fect	**A**ctive **M**iddle **P**assive	**P**articiple	**N**ominative **G**enitive **D**ative **A**ccusative	**S**ingular **P**lural	**M**asculine **F**eminine **N**euter

Let's learn how to recognize each of these pieces of the participle. Then we will put them into play.

Tense

Present tense is recognized the same way it always is. The clue is that there is no clue. Since we learn the present tense when we learn the verb, the present tense stem will be there smiling at you, shouting "Hey! I'm present tense!"

Voice

This is easier than you might think. Notice that the middle/passive forms all have μεν after the connecting vowel. This is a sure sign that a participle is middle or passive. It's worth repeating:

μεν
in the middle
is a sure sign that you're looking at a
middle/passive participle.

By process of elimination, if the participle lacks μεν, you can assume it is active. But that is a backwards way to identify an active participle. Here is the positive approach.

Active participles all have either ντ or ουσα/η. Of the two, ντ is more common. So here is how to spot an active participle.

ντ and ουσα/η
are dead giveaways
that you are looking at an
active participle.

Case, Number, Gender

We find the case, number and gender exactly as we would expect — by the case endings. As we learned in the last lesson, since the participles are adjectival they have to be able to take on 24 forms.

Do you remember the 2-1-2 pattern of declension? It is the most common way that adjectives decline. The article, for example, follows this pattern. It means the adjective follows:

➡ Second declension in the masculine gender
➡ First declension in the feminine gender, and
➡ Second declension in the neuter gender

Then, there was the 3-1-3 pattern of declension. The adjective πᾶς followed this pattern. It followed:

➡ Third declension in the masculine gender
➡ First declension in the feminine gender, and
➡ Third declension in the neuter gender

<u>We have seen it all before.</u> You should be nodding off on me!

If you remember these patterns, you will have no problem with participles. If not, you might want to go back and re-watch videos 12 and 13.

Here's the rule:

Present active participles follow the 3-1-3 pattern of declension.
Present, Middle/Passive participles follow the 2-1-2 pattern of declension.

To illustrate…

Comparison of the present active participle and πάς

active ντ, ουσα, ντ 3-1-3		
M (3)	**F (1)**	**N (3)**
λύων	λύουσα	λῦον
λύοντος	λυούσης	λύοντος
λύοντι	λυούσῃ	λύοντι
λύοντα	λύουσαν	λῦον
λύοντες	λύουσαι	λύοντα
λυόντων	λυουσῶν	λυόντων
λύουσιν	λυούσαις	λύουσιν
λύοντας	λύουσας	λύοντα

24 forms of πας (3-1-3)			
	3 masc	**I fem**	**3 neut**
N	πας	πασα	παν
G	παντος	πασης	παντος
D	παντι	παση	παντι
A	παντα	πασαν	παν
N	παντες	πασαι	παντα
G	παντων	πασων	παντων
D	πασι[ν]	πασαις	πασι[ν]
A	παντας	πασας	παντα

You will want to note the nominative, singular, masculine form (ων, shaded yellow in the chart above). This is an exception to the rule, but we are used to nominative forms being odd.

Comparison of the present, middle/passive participle and the article

middle passive μενο, μενη, μενο 2-1-2		
M (2)	**F (1)**	**N (2)**
λυόμενος	λυομένη	λυόμενον
λυομένου	λυομένης	λυομένου
λυομένῳ	λυομένη	λυομένῳ
λυόμενον	λυομένην	λυόμενον
λυόμενοι	λυόμεναι	λυόμενα
λυομένων	λυομένων	λυομένων
λυομένοις	λυομέναις	λυομένοις
λυομένους	λυομένας	λυόμενα

The Article				M (2)	F (1)	N (2)
Singular	Nominative	"the"		ὁ	ἡ	τό
	Genitive	"of the"		τοῦ	τῆς	τοῦ
	Dative	"to the"		τῷ	τῇ	τῷ
	Accusative	the		τόν	τήν	τό
Plural	Nominative	"the"		οἱ	αἱ	τά
	Genitive	"of the"		τῶν	τῶν	τῶν
	Dative	"to the"		τοῖς	ταῖς	τοῖς
	Accusative	"the"		τούς	τάς	τά

The bottom line: If you understand how the 2-1-2 and 3-1-3 adjective behaves, you can easily tell the case, number, and gender of a participle.

Let's Practice

Here are a few examples to demonstrate.

πιστευομένην

(being believed)

Let's break it into pieces to examine it.

πιστευ ο μέν ην

➡ The stem has not changed from what we learned (πιστεύ). It is present tense.

➡ It contains μεν so it is either middle or passive voice. (ο is the connecting vowel.)

➡ ην is the accusative, singular feminine noun ending.

So to parse πιστευομένην we simply describe it as a present, middle/passive participle, accusative, singular, feminine.

One more for good measure.

καταβαίνοντα

(going down)

Let's break it into pieces.

καταβαίν ο ντ α

➡ The stem has not changed from what we learned (καταβαιν). It is present tense.

➡ It contains ντ so it is active voice. (ο is the connecting vowel.)

➡ α is the nominative or accusative, plural neuter noun ending for the third declension.

So to parse καταβαίνοντα we simply describe it as a present, active participle, nominative or accusative, plural, neuter.

That is how you parse a present participle.

Now let's look at some participles in sentences.

How To Use The Present Participle

Adjectival Participle

Ἴδε ὁ ἀμνὸς τοῦ θεοῦ ὁ αἴρων τὴν ἁμαρτίαν τοῦ κόσμου.
Behold the lamb   *   of God   taking away the   sin   of the   world.

αἴρων is a present, active participle, nominative, singular, masculine.

★ αἴρων is adjectival. It modifies ὁ ἀμνὸς τοῦ θεοῦ.

★ Often with Greek adjectival participles, you have to add some words to smooth things out. Usually this is translated, "Behold, the Lamb of God who takes away the sin of the world." It is better English. But the present force of the participle gets lost.

★ The case, number and gender of the participle match the case, number and gender of the noun being modified (ὁ ἀμνὸς).

★ The underlined words are the participial phrase.

★ IMPORTANT: The adjectival participle almost always has the article.

Substantival Participle

οἱ πιστεύοντες σωθήσονται.
The   believing (ones)   will be saved.

πιστεύοντες is a present, active participle, nominative, plural, masculine.

★ πιστεύοντες is substantival. It does not modify anything. I put "ones" in parentheses. Often with Greek substantivals you have to add the implied subject in your English translation.

★ The case, number and gender match the plural subject. (Those who will be saved.)

★ The underlined words are the participial phrase.

★ IMPORTANT: The substantival participle almost always has the article.

Adverbial Participle

ταῦτα εἶπεν ἐν συναγωγῇ διδάσκων ἐν Καφαρναούμ.

these (things) he said   in   the synagogue   teaching   in   Capernaum.

διδάσκων is a present, active participle, nominative, singular, masculine.

- ★ διδάσκων is adverbial. It tells us more about εἶπεν.
- ★ The case, number and gender match the "he" in "he said."
- ★ The underlined words are the participial phrase.
- ★ IMPORTANT: The adverbial participle **never** has the article.

The best way — the only way — to learn these is to meet a bunch of them in context. Try your hand at translating the sentences in the workbook.

Do not become discouraged if you find these difficult. You will get the hang of it!

36. Aorist Participles

Lesson in a Nutshell

Aorist participles are based on the de-augmented aorist tense stem.

- Active voice will contain ντ or σασα. They follow the 3-1-3 pattern.
- Middle voice will contain μεν. They follow the 2-1-2 pattern.
- Passive voice will contain θε. They follow the 3-1-3 pattern.

Aorist participles convey undefined aspect.

In this chapter, we will learn how to recognize and translate aorist participles. Let's begin with recognition.

How To Parse an Aorist Participle

Aorist Participles								
active ντ, σασα, ντ 3-1-3			middle μενο, μενη, μενο 2-1-2			passive θεντ, θεισα, θεντ 3-1-3		
M (3)	F (1)	N (3)	M (2)	F (1)	N (2)	M (3)	F (1)	N (3)
λύσας	λύσασα	λῦσαν	λυσάμενος	λυσαμένη	λυσαμένων	λυθείς	λυθεῖσα	λυθέν
λύσαντος	λυσάσης	λύσαντος	λυσαμένου	λυσαμένης	λυσαμένου	λυθέντος	λυθείσης	λυθέντος
λύσαντι	λυσάσῃ	λύσαντι	λυσαμένῳ	λυσαμένῃ	λυσαμένῳ	λυθέντι	λυθείσῃ	λυθέντι
λύσαντα	λύσασαν	λῦσαν	λυσάμενον	λυσαμένην	λυσάμενον	λυθέντα	λυθεῖσαν	λυθέν
λύσαντες	λύσασαι	λύσαντα	λυσάμενοι	λυσάμεναι	λυσάμενα	λυθέντες	λυθεῖσαι	λυθέντα
λυσάντων	λυσασῶν	λυσάντων	λυσαμένων	λυσαμένων	λυσαμένων	λυθέντων	λυθέντων	λυθέντων
λύσασιν	λυσάσαις	λύσασιν	λυσαμένοις	λυσαμέναις	λυσαμένοις	λυθεῖσιν	λυθείσαις	λυθεῖσιν
λύσαντας	λυσάσας	λύσαντα	λυσαμένους	λυσαμένας	λυσάμενα	λυθέντας	λυθείσας	λυθέντα

Second Aorist Participles								
active ντ, ουσα, ντ 3-1-3			middle μενο, μενη, μενο 2-1-2			passive εντ, εισα, εντ 3-1-3		
M (3)	F (1)	N (3)	M (2)	F (1)	N (2)	M (2)	F (1)	N (2)
βαλών	βαλοῦσα	βαλόν	βαλόμενος	βαλομένη	βαλόμενον	γραφείς	γραφεῖσα	γραφέν
βαλόντος	βαλούσης	βαλόντος	βαλομένου	βαλομένης	βαλομένου	γραφέντος	γραφείσης	γραφέντος
βαλόντι	βαλούσῃ	βαλόντι	βαλομένῳ	βαλομένῃ	βαλομένῳ	γραφέντι	γραφείσῃ	γραφέντι
βαλόντα	βαλοῦσαν	βαλόν	βαλόμενον	βαλομένην	βαλόμενον	γραφέντα	γραφεῖσαν	γραφέν
βαλόντες	βαλοῦσαι	βαλόντα	βαλόμενοι	βαλόμεναι	βαλόμενα	γραφέντες	γραφεῖσαι	γραφέντα
βαλόντων	βαλουσῶν	βαλόντων	βαλομένων	βαλομένων	βαλομένων	γραφέντων	γραφεισῶν	γραφέντων
βαλοῦσιν	βαλούσαις	βαλοῦσιν	βαλομένοις	βαλομέναις	βαλομένοις	γραφεῖσιν	γραφείσαις	γραφεῖσιν
βαλόντας	βαλούσας	βαλόντα	βαλομένους	βαλομένας	βαλόμενα	γραφέντας	γραφείσας	γραφέντα

Once again, the sheer number of forms may cause an allergic reaction! Hopefully by now you're seeing that there are only a few patterns behind all these forms.

 Remember: We are just trying to discover the tense and voice, case, number and gender.

Before going on, look at the Aorist Participle table. How many patterns can you already recognize?

Tense

Aorist tense is recognized in the ways we have already learned.

➡ σα (active and middle) and θε[1] (passive) are the big giveaways for first aorists.

➡ The stem change is the giveaway for second aorists.

Voice

We recognize the voice from the participle morpheme. Most of these forms are similar to forms we already know.

➡ Active: ντ or σασα (ουσα in the second aorist).

➡ Middle: μεν.

➡ Passive: θε (just ε in the second aorist passive).

Case, Number, Gender

Aorist active participles follow the 3-1-3 pattern of declension.

Aorist middle participles follow the 2-1-2 pattern of declension.

Aorist passive participles follow the 3-1-3 pattern of declension.

---

[1] In the participle it is θε, rather than θη, as we have come to expect everywhere else.

At the risk of being too repetitive, here is a comparison with πᾶς (which follows the 3-1-3 pattern), and the article (which follows the 2-1-2 pattern).

Comparison of the aorist active participle with πᾶς

(after) loosing ντ, σασα		
M (3)	F (1)	N (3)
λύσας	λύσασα	λῦσαν
λύσαντος	λυσάσης	λύσαντος
λύσαντι	λυσάσῃ	λύσαντι
λύσαντα	λύσασαν	λῦσαν
λύσαντες	λύσασαι	λύσαντα
λυσάντων	λυσασῶν	λυσάντων
λύσασιν	λυσάσαις	λύσασιν
λύσαντας	λυσάσας	λύσαντα

24 forms of πᾶς (3-1-3)			
	3 masc	1 fem	3 neut
N	πας	πασα	παν
G	παντος	πασης	παντος
D	παντι	πασῃ	παντι
A	παντα	πασαν	παν
N	παντες	πασαι	παντα
G	παντων	πασων	παντων
D	πασι[ν]	πασαις	πασι[ν]
A	παντας	πασας	παντα

Comparison of the aorist middle participle with the article

middle σαμενο, σαμενη, σαμενο 2-1-2		
M (2)	F (1)	N (2)
λυσάμενος	λυσαμένη	λυσαμένων
λυσαμένου	λυσαμένης	λυσαμένου
λυσαμένῳ	λυσαμένῃ	λυσαμένῳ
λυσάμενον	λυσαμένην	λυσάμενον
λυσάμενοι	λυσάμεναι	λυσάμενα
λυσαμένων	λυσαμένων	λυσαμένων
λυσαμένοις	λυσαμέναις	λυσαμένοις
λυσαμένους	λυσαμένας	λυσάμενα

The Article				
			M (2)	F (1)	N (2)
Singular	Nominative "the"	ὁ	ἡ	τό
	Genitive "of the"	τοῦ	τῆς	τοῦ
	Dative "to the"	τῷ	τῇ	τῷ
	Accusative the	τόν	τήν	τό
Plural	Nominative "the"	οἱ	αἱ	τά
	Genitive "of the"	τῶν	τῶν	τῶν
	Dative "to the"	τοῖς	ταῖς	τοῖς
	Accusative "the"	τούς	τάς	τά

Comparison of the aorist passive participle with πᾶς

(after) being loosed θεντ, θεισα		
M (3)	F (1)	N (3)
λυθείς	λυθεῖσα	λυθέν
λυθέντος	λυθείσης	λυθέντος
λυθέντι	λυθείσῃ	λυθέντι
λυθέντα	λυθεῖσαν	λυθέν
λυθέντες	λυθεῖσαι	λυθέντα
λυθέντων	λυθέντων	λυθέντων
λυθεῖσιν	λυθείσαις	λυθεῖσιν
λυθέντας	λυθείσας	λυθέντα

24 forms of πᾶς (3-1-3)			
	3 masc	1 fem	3 neut
N	πας	πασα	παν
G	παντος	πασης	παντος
D	παντι	πασῃ	παντι
A	παντα	πασαν	παν
N	παντες	πασαι	παντα
G	παντων	πασων	παντων
D	πασι[ν]	πασαις	πασι[ν]
A	παντας	πασας	παντα

Let's Practice

Here are a few examples to demonstrate.

$$\pi\iota\sigma\tau\varepsilon\upsilon\sigma\alpha\nu\tau\varepsilon\varsigma$$
(believing)

Let's break it into pieces to examine.

$$\pi\iota\sigma\tau\varepsilon\upsilon \; \sigma\alpha \; \nu\tau \; \varepsilon\varsigma$$

➡ $\sigma\alpha$ tells me this must be an aorist participle.

➡ $\nu\tau$ tells me this is an active participle.

➡ $\varepsilon\varsigma$ is the nominative plural, masculine case ending in the third declension.

So to parse $\pi\iota\sigma\tau\varepsilon\upsilon\sigma\alpha\nu\tau\varepsilon\varsigma$ we simply describe it as an aorist, active participle, nominative, plural, masculine.

Here's another:

$$\pi\iota\sigma\tau\varepsilon\upsilon\sigma\acute{\alpha}\mu\varepsilon\nu\alpha\iota$$
(believing *for self*)

breaking it into pieces…

$$\pi\iota\sigma\tau\varepsilon\upsilon \; \sigma\acute{\alpha} \; \mu\varepsilon\nu \; \alpha\iota$$

➡ $\sigma\alpha$ tells me this must be an aorist participle.

➡ $\mu\varepsilon\nu$ tells me this is a middle participle.

➡ $\alpha\iota$ is the nominative plural, feminine case ending in the second declension.

So to parse $\pi\iota\sigma\tau\varepsilon\upsilon\sigma\acute{\alpha}\mu\varepsilon\nu\alpha\iota$ we simply describe it as an aorist, middle participle, nominative, plural, feminine.

Base Camp

Know your ABC's

1. Grammar Overview

Lesson in a Nutshell

The parts of speech may be divided into substance, motion, and relationship.
  a. Substance
      i. nouns (persons, places and things)
      ii. articles ("the" and "a" in English)
      iii. adjectives (modify nouns)
      iv. pronouns (stand in for nouns)
  b. Motion
      i. verbs (action words)
      ii. adverbs (modify verbs)
      iii. participles (verbal adjectives)
      iv. infinitives (verbal nouns)
  c. Relationship
      i. prepositions (anything you can do with a box)
      ii. conjunctions (connect words and phrases and clauses)

Close your eyes.

Now open them.

What do you see?

To answer this question you will use language. Language is fascinating.

But language is not reality.

Language is just a series of arbitrary noises we make and attach to reality. Say the word "monkey," for example. A long time ago we English speakers agreed that this strange sound would call to mind the furry critter that lives in trees and swings by its tail. But this is only true in English. Saying the word "monkey" in China would be as meaningless as saying the word "Hou-Zi" in America.

There are patterns that every language follows. These patterns are called grammar.

We will break grammar into three categories: Substance, Motion, and Relationship.

Adverbial Participle

ἐλθόντες εἰς τὴν οἰκίαν εἶδον τὸ παιδίον.

coming   into   the   house,   they saw   the   child.

ἐλθόντες is a (second) aorist, active participle, nominative, plural, masculine (from ἔρχομαι).

- ★ ἐλθόντες is adverbial. It tells us more about εἶδον.
- ★ The case, number and gender match "they" in "they saw."
- ★ The underlined words are the participial phrase.
- ★ IMPORTANT: The adverbial participle **never** has the article.

Now try your hand at translating the sentences in the workbook. Again, do not become discouraged if you find these difficult. You will get the hang of it!

37. Perfect Participles

Lesson in a Nutshell

Perfect participles are based on the perfect tense stem.

- Active voice will contain κοτ or κυια. They follow the 3-1-3 pattern.
- Middle/passive voice will contain μεν. They follow the 2-1-2 pattern.

Present participles convey perfected aspect.

In this chapter, we will learn how to recognize and translate perfect participles. Let's begin with recognition.

How To Parse a Perfect Participle

Perfect Participles					
active κοτ, κυια, κοτ 3-1-3			middle / passive μενο, μενη, μενο 2-1-2		
M (3)	F (1)	N (3)	M (2)	F (1)	N (2)
λελυκώς	λελυκυῖα	λελυκός	λελυμένος	λελυμένη	λελυμένον
λελυκότος	λελυκυίας	λελυκότος	λελυμένου	λελυμένης	λελυμένου
λελυκότι	λελυκυίᾳ	λελυκότι	λελυμένῳ	λελυμένῃ	λελυμένῳ
λελυκότα	λελυκυῖαν	λελυκός	λελυμένον	λελυμένην	λελυμένον
λελυκότες	λελυκυῖαι	λελυκότα	λελυμένοι	λελυμέναι	λελυμένα
λελυκότων	λελυκυιῶν	λελυκότων	λελυμένων	λελυμένων	λελυμένων
λελυκόσιν	λελυκυίαις	λελυκόσιν	λελυμένοις	λελυμέναις	λελυμένοις
λελυκότας	λελυκυίας	λελυκότα	λελυμένους	λελυμένας	λελυμένα

Hopefully by now, the number of forms does not even faze you. It is the same old routine, just a few patterns to notice, not dozens of forms to memorize.

Again, (and again and again) allow me to remind you that we are trying to discover the tense and voice, case, number and gender. We already know most of this.

Before turning the page, look at the Perfect Participle table and see how many patterns you can recognize.

Tense

Perfect tense is recognized in the ways we have already learned.

➡ reduplication!

➡ κ in the active and no connecting vowel in the middle / passive.

Voice

Once again, we recognize the voice from the participle morpheme.

➡ Active: κοτ or κυια

➡ Middle / Passive: μεν

Case, Number, Gender

Perfect <u>active</u> participles follow the 3-1-3 pattern of declension.

Perfect <u>middle / passive</u> participles follow the 2-1-2 pattern of declension.

I am really overdoing it, but here is a comparison with πᾶς and the article. Concentrate on the endings. I am trying to drive home the point that these endings are everywhere, and that you already know them.

<u>Comparison of the perfect active participle with πᾶς</u>

active κοτ, κυια, κοτ 3-1-3		
M (3)	**F (1)**	**N (3)**
λελυκώς	λελυκυῖα	λελυκός
λελυκότος	λελυκυίας	λελυκότος
λελυκότι	λελυκυίᾳ	λελυκότι
λελυκότα	λελυκυῖαν	λελυκός
λελυκότες	λελυκυῖαι	λελυκότα
λελυκότων	λελυκυιῶν	λελυκότων
λελυκόσιν	λελυκυίαις	λελυκόσιν
λελυκότας	λελυκυίας	λελυκότα

24 forms of πας (3-1-3)			
	3 masc	**I fem**	**3 neut**
N	πας	πασα	παν
G	παντος	πασης	παντος
D	παντι	παση	παντι
A	παντα	πασαν	παν
N	παντες	πασαι	παντα
G	παντων	πασων	παντων
D	πασι[v]	πασαις	πασι[v]
A	παντας	πασας	παντα

Comparison of the perfect middle / passive participle with the article

middle / passive μενο, μενη, μενο 2-1-2		
M (2)	**F (1)**	**N (2)**
λελυμένος	λελυμένη	λελυμένον
λελυμένου	λελυμένης	λελυμένου
λελυμένῳ	λελυμένῃ	λελυμένῳ
λελυμένον	λελυμένην	λελυμένον
λελυμένοι	λελυμέναι	λελυμένα
λελυμένων	λελυμένων	λελυμένων
λελυμένοις	λελυμέναις	λελυμένοις
λελυμένους	λελυμένας	λελυμένα

The Article					
			M (2)	**F (1)**	**N (2)**
Singular	Nominative	"the"	ὁ	ἡ	τό
	Genitive	"of the"	τοῦ	τῆς	τοῦ
	Dative	"to the"	τῷ	τῇ	τῷ
	Accusative	the	τόν	τήν	τό
Plural	Nominative	"the"	οἱ	αἱ	τά
	Genitive	"of the"	τῶν	τῶν	τῶν
	Dative	"to the"	τοῖς	ταῖς	τοῖς
	Accusative	"the"	τούς	τάς	τά

Let's Practice

Here are a few examples to demonstrate.

πεπιστευκότες
(having believed)

Let's break it into pieces to examine.

πε πιστευ κότ ες

➡ The reduplication and κ tell me it is perfect tense.

➡ κοτ tells me this is an active participle.

➡ ες is the nominative plural, masculine case ending in the third declension.

So to parse πεπιστευκότες we describe it as a perfect, active participle, nominative, plural, masculine.

Here's another:

$$\pi\epsilon\pi\iota\sigma\tau\epsilon\upsilon\mu\acute{\epsilon}\nu o\varsigma$$

(having been believed)

breaking it into pieces…

$$\pi\epsilon \ \pi\iota\sigma\tau\epsilon\upsilon \ \mu\acute{\epsilon}\nu \ o\varsigma$$

➡ The reduplication tells me this is perfect tense.

➡ μεν tells me this is a middle / passive participle.

➡ oς is the nominative singular, masculine case ending in the second declension.

So to parse πεπιστευμένος we describe it as a perfect, middle or passive participle, nominative, singular, masculine.

That is how you parse a perfect participle.

Now let's look at some perfect participles in sentences.
Remember that the only difference in meaning will be that of aspect.

How To Use The Perfect Participle

Adjectival Participle

ὁ ἄνθρωπος ὁ γεγεννημένος ἐκ τοῦ θεοῦ ἁμαρτίαν οὐ ποιεῖ.
the   man   *   having been born   from   *   God   sin   not he practices.

γεγεννημένος is a perfect, passive participle, nominative, singular, masculine (from γεννάω).

★ γεγεννημένος is adjectival. It modifies ὁ ἄνθρωπος.
★ The case, number and gender of the participle match the case, number and gender of the noun being modified (ὁ ἀνήρ).
★ The underlined words are the participial phrase.
★ IMPORTANT: The adjectival participle almost always has the article.

Substantival Participle

ὁ γεγεννημένος <u>ἐκ τοῦ θεοῦ</u> ἁμαρτίαν οὐ ποιεῖ.

The   having been born   from   *   God   sin   not he practices.

= The (one who) has been born from   *   God   sin   not he practices.

γεγεννημένος is a perfect, passive participle, nominative, singular, masculine.

- ★ γεγεννημένος is substantival. There is no noun to modify.
- ★ The case, number and gender match the implied subject. (The man[1] who has been born of God.)
- ★ The smoothed out version adds the implied subject. This is a legitimate translation.
- ★ The underlined words are the participial phrase.
- ★ IMPORTANT: The substantival participle almost always has the article.

Adverbial Participle

Ἐγένετο ἄνθρωπος <u>ἀπεσταλμένος παρὰ θεοῦ</u>.

came   a man   having been sent   from   God.

ἀπεσταλμένος is a perfect, passive participle, nominative, singular, masculine (from ἀποστέλλω).

- ★ ἀπεσταλμένος is adverbial. It tells us more about Ἐγένετο.
- ★ The case, number and gender match ἄνθρωπος.
- ★ The underlined words are the participial phrase.
- ★ IMPORTANT: The adverbial participle **never** has the article.

Now try your hand at translating the sentences in the workbook. Again, do not become discouraged if you find these difficult. Remember, this is your first semester of Greek!

---

[1] In this case the masculine form is gender inclusive, much in the same way as in older English "mankind" referred to all humanity, not just males.

Τετέλεσται

Printed in Great Britain
by Amazon

40745900R00126